NLN PAX Math
Workbook

PAX Math Exercises, Tutorials and
Multiple Choice Strategies

Copyright © 2022 by Complete Test Preparation Inc. ALL RIGHTS RESERVED.

No part of this book may be reproduced or transferred in any form or by any means, graphic, electronic, or mechanical, including photocopying, recording, web distribution, taping, or by any information storage retrieval system, without the written permission of the author.

Notice: Complete Test Preparation Inc. makes every reasonable effort to obtain from reliable sources accurate, complete, and timely information about the tests covered in this book. Nevertheless, changes can be made in the tests or the administration of the tests at any time and Complete Test Preparation Inc. makes no representation or warranty, either expressed or implied as to the accuracy, timeliness, or completeness of the information contained in this book. Complete Test Preparation Inc. make no representations or warranties of any kind, express or implied, about the completeness, accuracy, reliability, suitability or availability with respect to the information contained in this document for any purpose. Any reliance you place on such information is therefore strictly at your own risk.

The author(s) shall not be liable for any loss incurred as a consequence of the use and application, directly or indirectly, of any information presented in this work. Sold with the understanding, the author is not engaged in rendering professional services or advice. If advice or expert assistance is required, the services of a competent professional should be sought.

Please note that the PAX RN is administered by the National League of Nursing which is not involved in the production of, and does not endorse, this product.

We strongly recommend that students check with exam providers for up-to-date information regarding test content.

Published by
Complete Test Preparation Inc.
Victoria BC Canada

Visit us on the web at
https://www.test-preparation.ca
Printed in the USA

ISBN-13: 9781772451665

Version 8.5 Updated May 2022

About Complete Test Preparation

Why Us?
The Complete Test Preparation Team has been publishing high quality study materials since 2005, with a catalogue of over 145 titles, in English, French and Chinese, as well as ESL curriculum for all levels.

To keep up with the industry changes, we update everything all the time!

And the best part?
With every purchase, you're helping people all over the world improve themselves and their education. So thank you in advance for supporting this mission with us! Together, we are truly making a difference in the lives of those often forgotten by the system.

Charities that we support
https://www.test-preparation.ca/charities-and-non-profits/

You have definitely come to the right place.
If you want to spend your valuable study time where it will help you the most - we've got you covered today and tomorrow.

https://www.facebook.com/CompleteTestPreparation/

https://www.youtube.com/user/MrTestPreparation

Feedback

We welcome your feedback. Email us at feedback@test-preparation.ca with your comments and suggestions. We carefully review all suggestions and often incorporate reader suggestions into upcoming versions. As a Print on Demand Publisher, we update our products frequently.

Contents

8 **Getting Started**
　　The PAX Study Plan　　9
　　Making a Study Schedule　　12

15 **Basic Operations**
　　Practice Questions　　17
　　Answer Key　　22

24 **Estimation**
　　Practice Questions　　27
　　Answer Key　　30

32 **Graphs and Tables**
　　Practice Questions　　34
　　Answer Key　　39

41 **Word Problems**
　　How to Solve Word Problems　　41
　　Types of Word Problems　　44
　　Answer Key　　66

75 **Fractions, Decimals and Percent**
　　Fraction Tips and Short-cuts　　75
　　Fractions Decimal & Percent　　75
　　Decimal Tips and Short-cuts　　81
　　Percent Tips, Tricks and Short-cuts 82
　　Practice Questions 86
　　Answer Key 93

98 **Metric Conversion**
　　Practice Questions　　102
　　Answer Key　　105

107 Basic Algebra
- Solving One-Variable Equations — 107
- Simplifying Polynomials — 108
- Factoring Polynomials — 109
- Quadratic Equations — 110
- Basic Algebra Practice — 113
- Answer Key — 121

136 Geometry
- Cartesian Plane, Grid and Plane — 136
- Pythagorean Geometry — 142
- Quadrilaterals — 145
- Geometry Practice Questions — 149
- Answer Key — 166

177 Speed, Force and Momentum
- Practice Questions — 182
- Answer Key — 185

187 Mode, Mean and Median
- Practice Questions — 190
- Answer Key — 193

195 Basic Math Multiple Choice

201 How to Study for a Math Test

205 How to Prepare for a Test

211 How to Take a Test
- Reading the Instructions — 203
- How to Take a Test - The Basics — 205
- In the Test Room — 209
- Avoid Anxiety Before a Test — 215
- Common Test-Taking Mistakes — 217

228 Conclusion

Getting Started

CONGRATULATIONS! By deciding to take the NLN PAX, you have taken the first step toward a great future! Of course, there is no point in taking this important examination unless you intend to do your best to earn the highest grade that you possibly can. That means getting yourself organized and discovering the best approaches, methods and strategies to master the material. Yes, that will require real effort and dedication on your part, but if you are willing to focus your energy and devote the study time necessary, before you know it you will be opening that letter of acceptance to the school of your dreams.

We know that taking on a new endeavor can be scary, and it is easy to feel unsure of where to begin. That's where we come in. This study guide is designed to help you improve your test-taking skills, show you a few tricks of the trade and increase both your competency and confidence.

NLN PAX Math Content

The Mathematics section contains:

- Basic operations - adding subtracting, multiplying and dividing whole numbers
- Median and mode
- Exponents

- Word problems
- Simple geometry
- Operations with polynomials
- Quadratics
- Ratio and proportion
- Fractions, decimals and percent
- Speed, acceleration and momentum

The PAX Study Plan

Now that you have made the decision to take the PAX, it's time to get started. Before you do another thing, you will need to figure out a plan of attack. The best study tip is to start early! The longer the time period you devote to regular study practice, the more likely you will retain the material and be able to reach it quickly. If you thought that 1 x 20 is the same as 2 x 10, guess what? It really is not, when it comes to study time. Reviewing material for just an hour per day over the course of 20 days is far better than studying for two hours a day for only 10 days. The more often you revisit a particular piece of information, the better you will know it. Not only will your grasp and understanding improve, but your ability to reach into your brain and quickly and efficiently pull out the tidbit you need, will be greatly enhanced as well.

The great Chinese scholar and philosopher Confucius believed that true knowledge could be defined as knowing what you know and what you do not know. The first step in preparing for the PAX Exam is to assess your strengths and weaknesses. You may already have an idea of what you know and what you do not know, but evaluating yourself for each of the math areas will clarify the details.

Making a Study Schedule

To make your study time the most productive, you will need to develop a study plan. The purpose of the plan is to organize all the bits of pieces of information in such a way that you will not feel overwhelmed. Rome was not built in a day, and learning everything you will need to know to pass the PAX Exam is going to take time, too. Arranging the material you need to learn into manageable chunks is the best way to go. Each study session should make you feel as though you have accomplished your goal, and your goal is simply to learn what you planned to learn during that particular session. Try to organize the content in such a way that each study session builds on previous ones. That way, you will retain the information, be better able to reach it, and review the previous bits and pieces at the same time.

The Best Study Tip! The best study tip is to start early! The longer you study regularly, the more you will retain and 'learn' the material. Studying for 1 hour per day for 20 days is far better than studying for 2 hours for 10 days.

What don't you know?

The first step is to assess your strengths and weaknesses. You may already have an idea of where your weaknesses are, or you can take our Self-assessment modules for each of the areas, math, English, science and reading.

Below is a table to assess your exam readiness in each content area. You can fill this in now, and correct if necessary after completing the self-assessments, or fill it in after you have taken the self-assessments.

Exam Readiness Assessment

Computation and Problem Solving	Rate 1 - 5
Basic Operations	
Basic Statistics	
Word Problems	
Basic Geometry	
Polynomials	
Quadratics	
Fractions, decimals and percent	
Speed, acceleration and momentum	
Estimation	
Metric Conversion	

Making a Study Schedule

The key to a study plan is to divide the material you need to learn into manageable size and learn it, while at the same time reviewing the material that you already know.

Using the table above, any scores of 3 or below, you need to spend time learning, going over, and practicing this subject area. A score of 4 means you need to review the material, but you don't have to spend time re-learning. A score of 5 and you are OK with just an occasional review before the exam.

A score of 0 or 1 means you really need to work on this area and should allocate the most time and the highest priority. Some students prefer a 5-day plan and others a 10-day plan. It also depends on how much time until the exam.

Here is an example of a 5-day plan based on an example from the table above:

> **Fractions, Decimals, Percent:** 1 Study 1 hour everyday – review on last day
> **Estimation:** 3 Study 1 hour for 2 days then ½ hour a day, then review
> **Basic Statistics:** 4 Review every second day
> **Metric Conversion:** 2 Study 1 hour on the first day – then ½ hour everyday
> **Interpret Graphs:** 5 Review for ½ hour every other day
> **Algebra:** 5 Review for ½ hour every other day
> **Word Problems:** 5 very confident – review a few times.

Using this example, here is a sample study plan which you can adapt to your own situation:

Day	Subject	Time
Monday		
Study	Fractions, Decimals, Percent	1 hour
Study	Metric Conversion	1 hour
	½ **hour break**	
Study	Estimation	1 hour
Review	Word Problems	½ hour
Tuesday		
Study	Fractions, Decimals, Percent	1 hour
Study	Metric Conversion	½ hour
	½ **hour break**	
Study	Data Interpretation	½ hour
Review	Basic Statistics	½ hour
Wednesday		
Study	Fractions, Decimals, Percent	1 hour
Study	Metric Conversion	½ hour
	½ **hour break**	
Study	Estimation	½ hour
Review	Word Problems	½ hour
Thursday		
Study	Fractions, Decimals, Percent	½ hour
Study	Metric Conversion	½ hour
Review	Estimation	½ hour

	½ hour break	
Review	Estimation	½ hour
Review	Basic Statistics	½ hour
Friday		
Review	Fractions, Decimals, Percent	½ hour
Review	Metric Conversion	½ hour
Review	Estimation	½ hour
	½ **hour break**	
Review	Basic Statistics	½ hour
Review	Metric Conversion	½ hour

Basic Operations

Basic Operations include the following:

- addition, subtraction, multiplication and division

- solve simple money problems

- identify numbers between 2 given numbers

- solve simple problems with positive and negative numbers.

Answer Sheet

	A	B	C	D
1	○	○	○	○
2	○	○	○	○
3	○	○	○	○
4	○	○	○	○
5	○	○	○	○
6	○	○	○	○
7	○	○	○	○
8	○	○	○	○
9	○	○	○	○
10	○	○	○	○
11	○	○	○	○
12	○	○	○	○
13	○	○	○	○
14	○	○	○	○
15	○	○	○	○
16	○	○	○	○
17	○	○	○	○
18	○	○	○	○
19	○	○	○	○
20	○	○	○	○

Practice Questions

1. 389 + 454 =

    a. 853
    b. 833
    c. 843
    d. 863

2. 9,177 + 7,204 =

    a. 16,4712
    b. 16,371
    c. 16,381
    d. 15,412

3. 8,390 - 5,239 =

    a. 3,261
    b. 3,151
    c. 3,161
    d. 3,101

4. 643 - 587 =

    a. 56
    b. 66
    c. 46
    d. 55

Basic Operations

5. 3,406 - 2,767 =

    a. 629
    b. 720
    c. 639
    d. 649

6. 149 × 7 =

    a. 1032
    b. 1043
    c. 1059
    d. 10

7. 309 × 17 =

    a. 5,303
    b. 4,913
    c. 4,773
    d. 5,253

8. 491 ÷ 9 =

    a. 54 r5
    b. 56 r6
    c. 57 r5
    d. 51 r

9. What is the best unit to measure the weight of a tanker truck?

    a. tons
    b. ounces
    c. quarts
    d. feet

10. What is the best unit to measure the length of a needle?

    a. centimeters

    b. feet

    c. ounces

    d. meters

11. What is the best unit to measure the depth of a lake?

    a. meters

    b. tons

    c. inches

    d. pounds

12. Jim bought $15.34 worth of candy and his sister bought $12.57 worth. How much less did his sister buy?

    a. 3.49

    b. 2.77

    c. 2.27

    d. 1.77

13. Andrea earned $877.20 on her summer vacation and Bill earned 107.82 less. How much did he earn?

    a. 107.48

    b. 459.44

    c. 789.38

    d. 769.38

14. 20% of the students in a class of 50 leave early. Half of the remaining students stay after class. The rest leave at the bell. How many students stay after class?

    a. 10
    b. 5
    c. 15
    d. 12

15. Which of the following is between 0.51 and 0.98?

    a. 0.75
    b. 0.25
    c. 0.45
    d. 0.99

16. Which of the following is between 0.0067 and 0.34?

    a. 0.078
    b. 0.42
    c. 0.0005
    c. 0.12

17. You are asked to calculate 40% of 250 and use the formula:

40/100 = X/250. What other equation could you use?

    a. 40X = 25000
    b. (40 * 250)/100
    c. (40 * 100)/250
    d. 100X = (40 * 250)

18. You are asked to calculate 1/3 of 150. Which of the following equations is correct?

    a. 3/150

    b. 150/3

    c. 150 * 3

    d. None of the above

19. -75 + (-14) =

    a. -99

    b. -89

    c. 89

    d. 99

20. 50 - (-22) =

    a. 28

    b. -28

    c. -72

    d. 72

Answer Key

1. C
389 + 454 = 843

2. C
9,177 + 7,204 = 16,381

3. B
8,390 - 5,239 = 3,151

4. A
643 - 587 = 56

5. C
3,406 - 2,767 = 639

6. B
149 × 7 = 1043

7. D
309 × 17 = 52,53

8. A
491 ÷ 9 = 54 r5

9. A
Tons are the best units to measure the weight of a tanker truck.

10. A
Centimeters are the best measure for the length of a needle.

11. A
Meters are the best measures for the depth of a lake.

12. B
She bought $2.77 less candy. 15.34 - 12.57 = 2.77

13. D
He earned 769.38 less than Andrea. 877.20 - 107.82 = 769.38.

14. B
20% of 50 = 10 students. Half stay after class, so 10/2 = 5.

15. A
0.75 is between 0.51 and 0.98.

16. A
0.078 is between 0.0067 and 0.34.

17. B
Another equation to calculate 40% of 250 is (40 * 250)/100.

18. B
The correct formula to calculate 1/3 of 150 is 150/3.

19. B
-75 + (-14) = -89

20. A
50 - (-22) = 28

Estimation

Here are some strategies for estimating answers.

Strategy 1: Break it down

Estimate 105 X 8

    a. 840
    b. 922
    c. 880
    d. 860

Answer: A
Break 105 into 2 parts: 100 and 5, then multiple both by 8, and add.

100 X 8 is easy - 100 X 8 = 800. And, 5 X 8 = 40, adding gives the answer, 840, Choice A

Strategy 2: Use base 10

Estimate 1050 x 128

    a. 210,000
    b. 200,000
    c. 21,000
    d. 130,000

1050 and 128 are difficult to multiply in your head so take 1000 and 100 - add two zeros to 1000 for the answer, 100,000. Because we rounded down to 1000 and 100, this estimate will be lower than the actual answer.

Looking at the choices, A, B and C can all be eliminated as too small (C) or too large (A and B) so the answer much be D.

Confirming with a calculator, 1050 X 128 = 134,400.

Answer Sheet

	A	B	C	D
1	○	○	○	○
2	○	○	○	○
3	○	○	○	○
4	○	○	○	○
5	○	○	○	○
6	○	○	○	○
7	○	○	○	○
8	○	○	○	○
9	○	○	○	○
10	○	○	○	○

Practice Questions

1. Brad has agreed to buy everyone a Coke. Each drink costs $1.89, and there are 5 friends. Estimate Brad's cost.

    a. $7
    b. $8
    c. $10
    d. $12

2. What is the best approximate solution for 1.135 - 113.5?

    a. -110
    b. 100
    c. -90
    d. 110

3. Estimate 16 x 230

    a. 31,000
    b. 301,000
    c. 3,100
    d. 3,000,000

4. Estimate 215 x 65

    a. 1,350
    b. 13,500
    c. 103,500
    d. 3,500

Estimation

5. Estimate 2009 x 108

   a. 110,000
   b. 200,000
   c. 21,000
   d. 210,000

6. Estimate 46,227 + 101,032

   a. 14,700
   b. 147,000
   c. 14,700,000
   d. 104,700

7. Estimate 4,210,987 – 210,078

   a. 4,000,000
   b. 40,000,000
   c. 400,000
   d. 40,000

8. Estimate 5205 / 25

   a. 108
   b. 308
   c. 208
   d. 408

9. Estimate 2045 / 15

   a. 140
   b. 1500
   c. 105
   d. 350

10. Estimate 136 / 12

    a. 10
    b. 11
    c. 12
    d. 13

Answer Key

1. C
If there are 5 friends, and each drink costs $1.89, we can round up to $2 per drink and estimate the total cost at, 5 X $2 = $10. The actual cost is 5 X $1.89 = $9.45.

2. A
1.135 -113.5 = -112.37. Best approximate = -110

3. C
16 X 230 = 3680
To estimate, break 16 into 10 and 6. 10 * 230 = 2300, and 6 * 230 will be about half that 1150 (actually 1380)

For an approximation, 2300 + 1150 = 3450. The only choice is choice C, 3100.

4. B
215 X 65 = 13975
Choices A (1,350) and D (3,500) can be eliminated right away as they are too small. Choice C (103,500) is too large and can be eliminated, leaving only choice B.

5. D
2009 * 108 = 216972
To estimate, use 2000 * 100, or add 2 zeros to 2000 for 200,000. The only choice that is close is choice D (210,000)

6. B
46,227 + 101,032 = 147,032
To estimate, use 50,000 + 100,000 = 150,000. The only choice close to 150,000 is choice B.

7. A
4,210,987 − 210,078
To estimate, use 4,000,000 and 200,000 = 3,800,000 and find the choice that is closest - choice A, 4,000,000

8. C
5205/25 = 208.2
To estimate, start with easy number, 1000 and divide by 25 = 40. Or, take 100 and divide by 25 = 4 and multiple by 10 get 1000/25.

so, if 1000/25 = 40, then multiple by 5 for 5000/25 = 200. The only choice close to 200 is choice C, 208.

9. A
2045 / 15 = 136.3333
To estimate, use 1000 / 10 = 100, which eliminates choice B and D. The two remaining choices are A and 140 and C 105. Looking at choice C, estimate 100 * 15 = 1500, which is too low, so the answer is choice A.

10. B
136/12 = 11.3333
To estimate, remember 12 X 12 = 144, so choices C and D can be eliminated. Choice A can be eliminated since 10 * 12 = 120, so the answer must be choice B

Graphs and Tables

Answer Sheet

	A	B	C	D
1	○	○	○	○
2	○	○	○	○
3	○	○	○	○
4	○	○	○	○
5	○	○	○	○
6	○	○	○	○
7	○	○	○	○
8	○	○	○	○
9	○	○	○	○
10	○	○	○	○

Practice Questions

1. Consider the graph above.

How many hospital visits per year does a person aged 85 or more make?

    a. 26.2

    b. 31.3

    c. More than 31.3

    d. A decision cannot be made from this graph.

2. Based on this graph, how many visits per year do you expect a person that is 95 or older to make?

    a. 31.3 or more

    b. Less than 31.3

    c. 31.3

    d. A decision cannot be made from this graph.

3. Consider the following population growth chart.

Country	Population 2000	Population 2005
Japan	122,251,000	128,057,000
China	1,145,195,000	1,341,335,000
United States	253,339,000	310,384,000
Indonesia	184,346,000	239,871,000

What country is growing the fastest?

   a. Japan

   b. China

   c. United States

   d. Indonesia

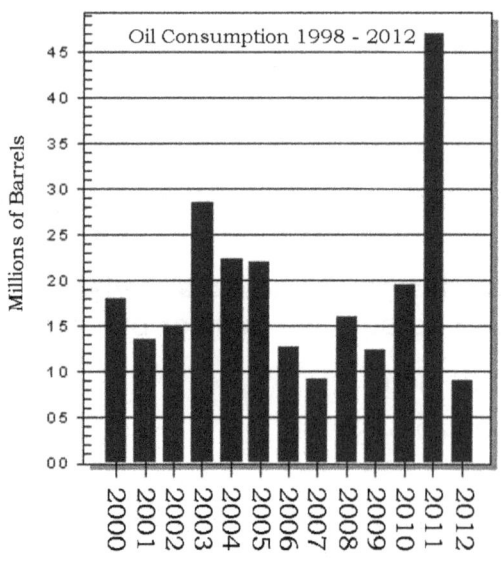

4. The graph above shows oil consumption in millions of barrels for the period, 1998 - 2012. What year did oil consumption peak?

   a. 2011
   b. 2010
   c. 2008
   d. 2009

5. Consider the graph above. What is the third best-selling product?

   a. Radar Detectors
   b. Flat Screen
   c. Blu Ray
   d. Auto CD Players

6. Which two products are the closest in the number of sales?

   a. Blu Ray and Flat Screen TV
   b. Flat Screen TV and Radar Detectors
   c. Radar Detectors and Auto CD Players
   d. DVD players and Blu Ray

7. According to the graph above, how many students received 62 or higher on the exam?

    a. 40
    b. 42
    c. 48
    d. 52

8. A girl has 4 red, 5 green and 2 yellow balls. She chooses two balls randomly. What is the probability that one is red and other is green?

    a. 2/11
    b. 19/22
    c. 20/121
    d. 9/11

In 2014, a survey is conducted to analyze the number of children in cities A and B. The table below shows the results of the study. The total population of city A is approximately 2 million, and the population of city B is 4 million.

	City A	City B
Less than 2 children	0.68	0.57
More than 2 and less than 4 children	0.29	0.42
More than 4 children	0.03	0.01
Total	1.00	1.00

9. According to the study, approximately how many residents have no children or 1 child in cities A and B?

    a. 1.2 million
    b. 1.36 million
    c. 2.28 million
    d. 3.64 million

Answer Key

1. A
Based on this graph, a person that is 85 or older will make 26.2 visits to the hospital every year.

2. A
A person aged 95 or older would make 31.3 or more visits.

3. D
Indonesia is growing the fastest, at about 30%.

4. A
According to the graph, oil consumption peaked in 2011.

5. B
Flat Screen TV are the third best-selling product.

6. B
The two products that are closest in the number of sales, are Flat Screen TVs and Radar Detectors.

7. B
42 students received a score of 62 or higher.

8. A
The probability that the 1st ball drawn is red = 4/11. The probability that the 2nd ball drawn is green = 5/10. The combined probability will then be 4/11 X 5/10 = 20/110 = 2/11.

9. D
The residents of city A have no children or 1 child.
In city B, 57% of the residents have no children or 1 child.

Since the total population is approximately 4 million; 2.28 million residents of city B have no children or 1 child.

Total: 1.36 + 2.28 = 3.64 million residents have no children or 1 child.

How to Solve Word Problems

Do you know what the biggest tip for solving word problems is?

Practice regularly and systematically.

Sounds simple and easy right? Yes it is, and yes it really does work.

Word problems are a way of thinking and require you to translate a real-world problem into mathematical terms.

Some math teachers say that learning how to think mathematically is the main reason for teaching word problems.

So what does that mean?

Studying word problems and math in general requires a logical and mathematical frame of mind. The only way you can get this is by practicing regularly, which means every day.

It is critical that you practice word problems every day for the 5 days before the exam as the absolute minimum.

If you practice and miss a day, you have lost the mathematical frame of mind and the benefit of your previous practice is gone. You must start all over again.

Word Problems

Everything is important.

All the information given in the problem has some purpose. There is no unnecessary information! Word problems are typically around 50 words in 2 or 3 sentences.

Often, the relationships are complicated. To explain everything, every word counts.

Make sure that you use every piece of information.

7 steps to solving word problems

Step 1 – Read through the problem at least three times. The first reading should be a quick scan, and the next two readings should be done slowly to find answers to these questions:

> What does the problem ask? (Usually located at the end)

Mark all information and underline all important words or phrases.

Step 2 – Draw a picture. Use arrows, circles, lines, whatever works for you. This makes the problem real.

A favorite word problem is something like, 1 train leaves Station A travelling at 100 km/hr and another train leaves Station B travelling at 60 km/hr. …

Draw a line, the two stations, and the two trains at either end.

Depending on the question, make a table with a blank portion to show information you don't know.

Step 3 – Assign a single letter to represent each unknown.

You may want to note the unknown that each letter

represents so you don't get confused.

Step 4 – Translate the information into an equation.

Remember that the main problem with word problems is that they are not expressed in regular math equations. Your ability to identify correctly the variables and translate the information into an equation determines your ability to solve the problem.

Step 5 – Check the equation to see if it looks like regular equations that you are used to seeing and whether it looks sensible.

Does the equation appear to represent the information in the question? Take note that you may need to rewrite some formulas needed to solve the word problem equation.

Step 6 – Use algebra rules to solve the equation.

Simplify each side of the equation by removing parentheses and combining like terms.

Use addition or subtraction to isolate the variable term on one side of the equation. If a number crosses to the other side of the equation, the sign changes to the opposite -- for example positive to negative.

Use multiplication or division to solve for the variable. What you to once side of the equation you must do for the other.

Where there are multiple unknowns you will need to use elimination or substitution methods to resolve all the equations.

Step 7 – Check your final answers to see if they make sense with the information given in the problem.

For example, if the word problem involves a discount, the final price should be less or if a product was taxed then the final answer has to cost more.

Types of Word Problems

Word problems can be classified into 12 types. Below are examples of each type with a complete solution. Some types of word problems can be solved quickly using multiple choice strategies and some cannot. Always look for ways to estimate the answer and then eliminate choices.

1. Age

A girl is 10 years older than her brother. By next year, she will be twice the age of her brother. What are their ages now?

    a. 25, 15
    b. 19, 9
    c. 21, 11
    d. 29, 19

Solution: B

We will assume that the girl's age is "a" and her brother's age is "b." This means that based on the information in the first sentence,
$a = 10 + b$

Next year, she will be twice her brother's age, which gives, $a + 1 = 2(b+1)$

We need to solve for one unknown factor and then use the answer to solve for the other. To do this we substitute the value of "a" from the first equation into the second equation. This gives

10+b + 1 = 2b + 2
11 + b = 2b + 2
11 − 2 = 2b − b
b = 9

9 = b this means that her brother is 9 years old. Solving for the girl's age in the first equation gives a = 10 + 9. a = 19 the girl is aged 19. So, the girl is aged 19 and the boy is 9

2. Distance or speed

Two boats travel down a river towards the same destination, starting at the same time. One is traveling at 52 km/hr, and the other boat at 43 km/hr. How far apart will they be after 40 minutes?

    a. 46.67 km
    b. 19.23 km
    c. 6.04 km
    d. 14.39 km

Solution: C

After 40 minutes, the first boat will have traveled = 52 km/hr x 40 minutes/60 minutes = 34.7 km
After 40 minutes, the second boat will have traveled = 43 km/hr x 40/60 minutes = 28.66 km
Difference between the two boats will be 34.7 km − 28.66 km = 6.04 km.

Multiple Choice Strategy

First estimate the answer. The first boat is traveling 9 km. faster than the second, for 40 minutes, which is 2/3 of an hour. 2/3 of 9 = 6, as a rough guess of the distance apart.

Choices A, B and D can be eliminated right away.

3. Ratio

The instructions in a cookbook state that 700 grams of flour must be mixed in 100 ml of water, and 0.90 grams of salt added. A cook however has just 325 grams of flour. What is the quantity of water and salt that he should use?

    a. 0.41 grams and 46.4 ml
    b. 0.45 grams and 49.3 ml
    c. 0.39 grams and 39.8 ml
    d. 0.25 grams and 40.1 ml

Solution: A

The Cookbook states 700 grams of flour, but the cook only has 325. The first step is to determine the percentage of flour he has $325/700 \times 100 = 46.4\%$
That means that 46.4% of all other items must also be used.
46.4% of 100 = 46.4 ml of water
46.4% of 0.90 = 0.41 grams of salt.

Multiple Choice Strategy

The recipe calls for 700 grams of flour but the cook only has 325, which is just less than half, the quantity of water and salt are going to be about half.

Choices C and D can be eliminated right away. Choice B is very close so be careful. Looking closely at choice B, it is exactly half, and since 325 is slightly less than half of 700, it can't be correct.

Choice A is correct.

4. Percent

An agent received $6,685 as his commission for selling a property. If his commission was 13% of the selling price, how much was the property?

    a. $68,825
    b. $121,850
    c. $49,025
    d. $51,423

Solution: D

Let's assume that the property price is x
That means from the information given, 13% of x = 6,685
Solve for x,
x = 6685 x 100/13 = $51,423

Multiple Choice Strategy

The commission, 13%, is just over 10%, which is easier to work with. Round up $6685 to $6700, and multiple by 10 for an approximate answer. 10 X 6700 = $67,000. You can do this in your head. Choice B is much too big and can be eliminated. Choice C is too small and can be eliminated. Choices A and D are left and good possibilities.

Do the calculations to make the final choice.

―― Word Problems ――

5. Sales & Profit

A store owner buys merchandise for $21,045. He transports them for $3,905 and pays his staff $1,450 to stock the merchandise on his shelves. If he does not incur further costs, how much does he need to sell the items to make $5,000 profit?

    a. $32,500
    b. $29,350
    c. $32,400
    d. $31,400

Solution: D

Total cost of the items is $21,045 + $3,905 + $1,450 = $26,400
Total cost is now $26,400 + $5000 profit = $31,400

Multiple Choice Strategy

Round off and add the numbers up in your head quickly. 21,000 + 4,000 + 1500 = 26500. Add in 5000 profit for a total of 31500.

Choice B is too small and can be eliminated. Choice C and choice A are too large and can be eliminated.

6. Tax/Income

A woman earns $42,000 per month and pays 5% tax on her monthly income. If the Government increases her monthly taxes by $1,500, what is her income after tax?

    a. $38,400
    b. $36,050
    c. $40,500
    d. $39, 500

Solution: A

Initial tax on income was 5/100 x 42,000 = $2,100
$1,500 was added to the tax to give $2,100 + 1,500 = $3,600
Income after tax is $42,000 - $3,600 = $38,400

7. Simple Interest Word Problems

Simple interest is one type of interest problems. There are always four variables of any simple interest equation. With simple interest, you would be given three of these variables and be asked to solve for one unknown variable. With more complex interest problems, you would have to solve for multiple variables.

The four variables of simple interest are:
    P – Principal which refers to the original amount of money put in the account
    I – Interest or the amount of money earned as interest
    r – Rate or interest rate. This MUST ALWAYS be in decimal format and not in percentage
    t – Time or the amount of time the money is kept in the account to earn interest

The formula for simple interest is $I = P \times r \times t$

Example 1

A customer deposits $1,000 in a savings account with a bank that offers 2% interest. How much interest will be earned after 4 years?

For this problem, there are 3 variables as expected.

P = $1,000
t = 4 years
r = 2%

I = ?
Before we can begin solving for I using the simple interest formula, we need to first convert the rate from percentage to decimal.

2% = 2/100 = 0.02
Now we can use the formula: I = P x r x t

I = 1,000 x 0.02 x 4 = 80
This means that the $1,000 would have earned an interest of $80 after 4 years. The total in the account after 4 years will thus be principal + interest earned, or 1,000 + 80 = $1,080

Example 2

Sandra deposits $1400 in a savings account with a bank at 5% interest. How long will she have to leave the money in the bank to earn $420 as interest to buy a second-hand car?

In this example, the given information is:
I = $420
P = $1,400
r - 5%
t - ?
As usual, first we convert the rate from percentage to decimal

5% = 5/100 = 0.05

Next, we plug in the variables we know into the simple interest formula - I = P x r x t

420 = 1,400 x 0.05 x t
420 = 70 x t
420 = 70t
t = 420/70
t = 6

Sandra will have to leave her $1,400 in the bank for 6 years to earn her an interest of $420 at a rate of 5%.

Other important simple interest formula to remember are below. To use these formula, do not convert r (rate) to decimal.

P = 100 x interest/ r x t
r = 100 x interest/p x t
t = 100 x interest/ p x r

8. Averaging

The average weight of 10 books is 54 grams. 2 more books were added and the average weight became 55.4. If one of the 2 new books added weighed 62.8 g, what is the weight of the other?

    a. 44.7 g
    b. 67.4 g
    c. 62 g
    d. 52 g

Solution: C

Total weight of 10 books with average 54 grams will be=10×54=540 g
Total weight of 12 books with average 55.4 will be=55.4×12=664.8 g
So total weight of the remaining 2 will be= 664.8 – 540 = 124.8 g
If one weighs 62.8, the weight of the other will be= 124.8 g – 62.8 g = 62 g

Multiple Choice Strategy

Averaging problems can be estimated by looking at which direction the average goes. If additional items are added and the average goes up, the new items much be greater than the average. If the average goes down after new items are added, the new items must be less than the average.

Here, the average is 54 grams and 2 books are added which increases the average to 55.4, so the new books must weight more than 54 grams.
Choices A and D can be eliminated right away.

9. Probability

A bag contains 15 marbles of various colors. If 3 marbles are white, 5 are red and the rest are black, what is the probability of randomly picking out a black marble from the bag?

    a. 7/15
    b. 3/15
    c. 1/5
    d. 4/15

Solution: A

Total marbles = 15
Number of black marbles = 15 − (3 + 5) = 7
Probability of picking out a black marble = 7/15

10. Two Variables

A company paid a total of $2850 to book 6 single rooms and 4 double rooms for one night. Another company paid $3185 to book for 13 single rooms for one night in the same hotel. What is the cost for single and double rooms in that hotel?

    a. single= $250 and double = $345
    b. single= $254 and double = $350
    c. single = $245 and double = $305
    d. single = $245 and double = $345

Solution: D

We can determine the price of single rooms from the information given of the second company. 13 single rooms = 3185.

One single room = 3185 / 13 = 245
The first company paid for 6 single rooms at $245. 245 x 6 = $1470

Total amount paid for 4 double rooms by first company = $2850 - $1470 = $1380

Cost per double room = 1380 / 4 = $345

11. Geometry

The length of a rectangle is 5 in. more than its width. The perimeter of the rectangle is 26 in. What is the width and length of the rectangle?

    a. width = 6 inches, Length = 9 inches
    b. width = 4 inches, Length = 9 inches
    c. width =4 inches, Length = 5 inches
    d. width = 6 inches, Length = 11 inches

Solution: B

Formula for perimeter of a rectangle is 2(L + W)
p=26, so 2(L+W) = p
The length is 5 inches more than the width, so
2(w+5) + 2w = 26
2w + 10 + 2w = 26
2w + 2w = 26 - 10
4w = 16

W = 16/4 = 4 inches

L is 5 inches more than w, so L = 5 + 4 = 9 inches.

12. Totals and fractions

A basket contains 125 oranges, mangoes and apples. If 3/5 of the fruits in the basket are mangoes and only 2/5 of the mangoes are ripe, how many ripe mangoes are there in the basket?

    a. 30
    b. 68
    c. 55
    d. 47

Solution: A
Number of mangoes in the basket is 3/5 x 125 = 75
Number of ripe mangoes = 2/5 x 75 = 30

Answer Sheet

	A	B	C	D	E		A	B	C	D	E
1	○	○	○	○	○	21	○	○	○	○	○
2	○	○	○	○	○	22	○	○	○	○	○
3	○	○	○	○	○	23	○	○	○	○	○
4	○	○	○	○	○	24	○	○	○	○	○
5	○	○	○	○	○	25	○	○	○	○	○
6	○	○	○	○	○						
7	○	○	○	○	○						
8	○	○	○	○	○						
9	○	○	○	○	○						
10	○	○	○	○	○						
11	○	○	○	○	○						
12	○	○	○	○	○						
13	○	○	○	○	○						
14	○	○	○	○	○						
15	○	○	○	○	○						
16	○	○	○	○	○						
17	○	○	○	○	○						
18	○	○	○	○	○						
19	○	○	○	○	○						
20	○	○	○	○	○						

Part 1 - Equation Translation

1. Translate the following into an equation: Five greater than 3 times a number.

    a. $3X + 5$
    b. $5X + 3$
    c. $(5 + 3)X$
    d. $5(3 + X)$

2. Translate the following into an equation: three plus a number times 7 equals 42.

    a. $7(3 + X) = 42$
    b. $3(X + 7) = 42$
    c. $3X + 7 = 42$
    d. $(3 + 7)X = 42$

3. Translate the following into an equation: 2 + a number divided by 7.

    a. $(2 + X)/7$
    b. $(7 + X)/2$
    c. $(2 + 7)/X$
    d. $2/(7 + X)$

4. Translate the following into an equation: six times a number plus five.

    a. $6X + 5$
    b. $6(X+5)$
    c. $5X + 6$
    d. $(6 * 5) + 5$

5. A box contains 7 black pencils and 28 blue ones. What is the ratio of black and blue pens?

   a. 1:4
   b. 2:7
   c. 1:8
   d. 1:9

6. The manager of a weaving factory estimates that if 10 machines run at 100% efficiency for 8 hours, they will produce 1450 meters of cloth. Due to some technical problems, 4 machines run of 95% efficiency and the remaining 6 at 90% efficiency. How many meters of cloth can these machines will produce in 8 hours?

   a. 1334 meters
   b. 1310 meters
   c. 1300 meters
   d. 1285 meters

7. In a local election at polling station A, 945 voters cast their vote out of 1270 registered voters. At polling station B, 860 cast their vote out of 1050 registered voters and at station C, 1210 cast their vote out of 1440 registered voters. What is the total turnout from all three polling stations?

   a. 70%
   b. 74%
   c. 76%
   d. 80%

8. If Lynn can type a page in p minutes, what portion of the page can she do in 5 minutes?

   a. p/5
   b. p - 5
   c. p + 5
   d. 5/p

9. If Sally can paint a house in 4 hours, and John can paint the same house in 6 hours, how long will it take for both to paint a house?

   a. 2 hours and 24 minutes
   b. 3 hours and 12 minutes
   c. 3 hours and 44 minutes
   d. 4 hours and 10 minutes

10. Employees of a discount appliance store receive an additional 20% off the lowest price on any item. If an employee purchases a dishwasher during a 15% off sale, how much will he pay if the dishwasher originally cost $450?

    a. $280.90
    b. $287.00
    c. $292.50
    d. $306.00

11. The sale price of a car is $12,590, which is 20% off the original price. What is the original price?

    a. $14,310.40
    b. $14,990.90
    c. $15,108.00
    d. $15,737.50

12. Richard gives 's' amount of salary to each of his 'n' employees weekly. If he has 'x' amount of money, how many days he can employ these 'n' employees.

   a. sx/7n
   b. 7x/nx
   c. nx/7s
   d. 7x/ns

13. A distributor purchased 550 pounds of potatoes for $165. He distributed these at a rate of $6.4 per 20 pounds to 15 shops, $3.4 per 10 pounds to 12 shops and the remainder at $1.8 per 5 pounds. If his total distribution cost is $10, what will his profit be?

   a. $10.40
   b. $8.60
   c. $14.90
   d. $23.40

14. How much pay does Mr. Johnson receive if he gives half of his pay to his family, $250 to his landlord, and has exactly 3/7 of his pay left over?

   a. $3600
   b. $3500
   c. $2800
   d. $1750

15. The cost of waterproofing canvas is .50 a square yard. What's the total cost for waterproofing a canvas truck cover that is 15' x 24'?

    a. $18.00
    b. $6.67
    c. $180.00
    d. $20.00

16. The price of a book went from $20 to $25. What percent did the price increase?

    a. 5%
    b. 10%
    c. 20%
    d. 25%

17. In the time required to serve 43 customers, a server breaks 2 glasses and slips 5 times. The next day, the same server breaks 10 glasses. Assuming that glasses broken is proportional to customers served, how many customers did she serve?

    a. 25
    b. 43
    c. 86
    d. 215

― Word Problems ―

18. A square lawn has an area of 62,500 square meters. What is the cost of building fence around it at a rate of $5.5 per meter?

    a. $4000
    b. $4500
    c. $5000
    d. $5500

19. Susan wants to buy a leather jacket that costs $545.00 and is on sale for 10% off. What is the approximate cost?

    a. $525
    b. $450
    c. $475
    d. $500

20. Sarah weighs 25 pounds more than Tony. If together they weigh 205 pounds, how much does Sarah weigh in kilograms? Assume 1 pound = 0.4535 kilograms.

    a. 41
    b. 48
    c. 50
    d. 52

21. A man buys an item for $420 and has a balance of $3000.00. How much did he have before his purchase?

    a. $2,580
    b. $3,420
    c. $2,420
    d. $342

22. The average weight of 13 students in a class of 15 (two were absent that day) is 42 kg. When the remaining two are weighed, the average became 42.7 kg. If one of the remaining students weighs 48 kg., how much does the other weigh?

    a. 44.7 kg.
    b. 45.6 kg.
    c. 46.5 kg.
    d. 47.4 kg.

23. The total expense of building a fence around a square-shaped field is $2000 at a rate of $5 per meter. What is the length of one side?

    a. 40 meters
    b. 80 meters
    c. 100 meters
    d. 320 meters

Word Problems

24. There were some oranges in a basket. By adding 8/5 of the total to the basket, the new total is 130. How many oranges were in the basket?

    a. 60
    b. 50
    c. 40
    d. 35

25. A person earns $25,000 per month and pays $9,000 income tax per year. The Government increased income tax by 0.5% per month and his monthly earning was increased $11,000. How much more income tax will he pay per month?

    a. $1260
    b. $1050
    c. $750
    d. $510

Answer Key

Part 1 - Equation Translation

1. A
Five greater than 3 times a number.
5 + 3 times a number.
3X + 5

2. A
Three plus a number times 7 equals 42.
Let X be the number.
(3 + X) times 7 = 42
7(3 + X) = 42

3. A
2 + a number divided by 7.
(2 + X) divided by 7.
(2 + X)/7

4. B
Six times a number plus five is the same as saying six times (a number plus five). Or,
6 * (a number plus five). Let X be the number so, 6(X+5).

5. A
The ratio between black and blue pens is 7 to 28 or 7:28. Bring to the lowest terms by dividing both sides by 7 gives 1:4.

6. A
At 100% efficiency 1 machine produces 1450/10 = 145 m of cloth.

At 95% efficiency, 4 machines produce 4 * 145 * 95/100 = 551 m of cloth.

At 90% efficiency, 6 machines produce 6 * 145 * 90/100 =

783 m of cloth.

Total cloth produced by all 10 machines = 551 + 783 = 1334 m

Since the information provided and the question are based on 8 hours, we did not need to use time to reach the answer.

7. D
To find the total turnout in all three polling stations, we need to proportion the number of voters to the number of all registered voters.

Number of total voters = 945 + 860 + 1210 = 3015

Number of total registered voters = 1270 + 1050 + 1440 = 3760

Percentage turnout over all three polling stations = 3015 * 100/3760 = 80.19%

Checking the answers, we round 80.19 to the nearest whole number: 80%

8. D
This is a simple direct proportion problem:
If Lynn can type 1 page in p minutes, then she can type x pages in 5 minutes

We do cross multiplication: x * p = 5 * 1

Then,

x = 5/p

9. A
This is an inverse ratio problem.

1/x = 1/a + 1/b where a is the time Sally can paint a

house, b is the time John can paint a house, x is the time Sally and John can together paint a house.

So,

$1/x = 1/4 + 1/6$ ... We use the least common multiple in the denominator that is 24:

$1/x = 6/24 + 4/24$

$1/x = 10/24$

$x = 24/10$

$x = 2.4$ hours.

In other words; 2 hours + 0.4 hours = 2 hours + 0.4 * 60 minutes

= 2 hours 24 minutes

10. D
The cost of the dishwasher = $450

15% discount amount = 450 * 15/100 = $67.5

The discounted price = 450 – 67.5 = $382.5

20% additional discount amount on lowest price = 382.5 * 20/100 = $76.5

So, the final discounted price = 382.5 - 76.5 = $306.00

11. D
Original price = x,
80/100 = 12590/X,
80X = 1259000,
X = 15,737.50.

12. D
We understand that each of the 'n' employees earn 's'

amount of salary weekly. This means that one employee earns 's' salary weekly. So; Richard has 'ns' amount of money to employ 'n' employees for a week.

We are asked to find the number of days n employees can be employed with x amount of money. We can do simple direct proportion:

If Richard can employ n employees for 7 days with 'ns' amount of money,

Richard can employ n employees for y days with x amount of money ... y is the number of days we need to find.

We can do cross multiplication:

y = (x * 7)/(ns)

y = 7x/ns

13. B

The distribution is done at three different rates and in three different amounts:

$6.4 per 20 kilograms to 15 shops ... 20 * 15 = 300 kilograms distributed

$3.4 per 10 kilograms to 12 shops ... 10 * 12 = 120 kilograms distributed

550 - (300 + 120) = 550 - 420 = 130 kilograms left. This amount is distributed in 5 kilogram portions. So, this means that there are 130/5 = 26 shops.

$1.8 per 130 kilograms.

We need to find the amount he earned overall these distributions.

$6.4 per 20 kilograms : 6.4 * 15 = $96 for 300 kilograms

$3.4 per 10 kilograms : 3.4 *12 = $40.8 for 120 kilograms

$1.8 per 5 kilograms : 1.8 * 26 = $46.8 for 130 kilograms

So, he earned 96 + 40.8 + 46.8 = $ 183.6

The total distribution cost is given as $10

The profit is found by: Money earned - money spent ... It is important to remember that he bought 550 kilograms of potatoes for $165 at the beginning:

Profit = 183.6 - 10 - 165 = $8.6

14. B
We check the fractions taking place in the question. We see that there is a "half" (that is 1/2) and 3/7. So, we multiply the denominators of these fractions to decide how to name the total money. We say that Mr. Johnson has 14x at the beginning; he gives half of this, meaning 7x, to his family. $250 to his landlord. He has 3/7 of his money left. 3/7 of 14x is equal to:

14x * (3/7) = 6x

So,

Spent money is: 7x + 250

Unspent money is: 6x

Total money is: 14x

Write an equation: total money = spent money + unspent money

14x = 7x + 250 + 6x

14x - 7x - 6x = 250

x = 250

We are asked to find the total money that is 14x:

14x = 14 * 250 = $3500

15. D
First calculate total square feet, which is 15 * 24 = 360 ft2. Next, convert this value to square yards, (1 yards2 = 9 ft2) which is 360/9 = 40 yards2. At $0.50 per square yard, the total cost is 40 * 0.50 = $20.

16. D
Price increased by $5 ($25-$20). To calculate the percent increase:
5/20 = X/100
500 = 20X
X = 500/20
X = 25%

17. D
2 glasses are broken for 43 customers so 1 glass breaks for every 43/2 customers served, therefore 10 glasses implies (43/2) * 10 = 215 customers.

18. D
As the lawn is square, the length of one side will be the square root of the area. √62,500 = 250 meters. So, the perimeter is found by 4 times the length of the side of the square:

250 * 4 = 1000 meters.

Since each meter costs $5.5, the total cost of the fence will be 1000 * 5.5 = $5,500.

19. D
The question asks for approximate cost, so work with round numbers. The jacket costs $545.00 so we can round up to $550. 10% of $550 is 55. We can round down to $50, which is easier to work with. $550 - $50 is

$500. The jacket will cost about $500.

The actual cost will be 10% X 545 = $54.50
545 − 54.50 = $490.50

20. D
Let us denote Sarah's weight by "x." Then, since she weighs 25 pounds more than Tony, Tony will be x-25. They together weigh 205 pounds which means that the sum of the two representations will be equal to 205:

Sarah : x

Tony : x - 25

x + (x - 25) = 205 ... by arranging this equation we have:

x + x - 25 = 205

2x - 25 = 205 ... we add 25 to each side in order to have x term alone:

2x - 25 + 25 = 205 + 25

2x = 230

x = 230/2

x = 115 pounds → Sarah weighs 115 pounds. Since 1 pound is 0.4535 kilograms, we need to multiply 115 by 0.4535 in order to have her weight in kilograms:

x = 115 * 0.4535 = 52.1525 kilograms → this is equal to 52 when rounded to the nearest whole number.

21. B
(Amount Spent) $420 + $3000 (Balance) = $3,420.00

22. C
Total weight of 13 students with average 42 will be = 42 *

13 = 546 kg.

The total weight of the remaining 2 will be found by subtracting the total weight of 13 students from the total weight of 15 students: 640.5 - 546 = 94.5 kg.

94.5 = the total weight of two students. One of these students weigh 48 kg, so;

The weight of the other will be = 94.5 – 48 = 46.5 kg

23. C
Total expense is $2000 and we are informed that $5 is spent per meter. Combining these two information, we know that the total length of the fence is 2000/5 = 400 meters.

The fence is built around a square-shaped field. If one side of the square is "a," the perimeter of the square is "4a." Here, the perimeter is equal to 400 meters. So,

400 = 4a

100 = a → this means that one side of the square is equal to 100 meters

24. B
Let the number of oranges in the basket before additions = x
Then: X + 8x/5 = 130
5x + 8x = 650
650 = 13x
X = 50

25. D
The income tax per year is $9,000. So, the income tax per month is 9,000/12 = $750.

This person earns $25,000 per month and pays $750

income tax. We need to find the rate of the income tax:

Tax rate: 750 * 100/25,000 = 3%
Government increased this rate by 0.5% so it became 3.5%.

The income of the person per month is increased $11,000 so it became:

$25,000 + $11,000 = $36,000.

The new monthly income tax is: 36,000 * 3.5/100 = $1260.

Amount of increase in tax per month is: $1260 - $750 = $510.

Fractions, Decimals & Percent

Basic math Video Tutorials

https://www.test-preparation.ca/math-videos/

Fraction Tips, Tricks and Short-cuts

When you are writing an exam, time is precious, so anything you can do to answer questions faster is a real advantage.

Here are some ideas, Short-cuts, tips and tricks that can speed up answering fraction problems.

Remember that a fraction is just a number which names a portion of something. For instance, instead of having a whole pie, a fraction says you have a part of a pie--such as a half of one or a fourth of one.

Two numbers make up a fraction. The number on top is the numerator. The number on the bottom is the denominator.

To remember which is which, just remember

that "denominator" and "down" both start with a "d." And the "downstairs" number is the denominator. So for instance, in ½, the numerator is 1, and the denominator (or "downstairs") number is 2.

Adding Fractions

It's easy to add two fractions if they have the same denominator. Just add the digits on top and leave the bottom one the same: 1/10 + 6/10 = 7/10.

It's the same with subtracting fractions with the same denominator: 7/10 - 6/10 = 1/10.

Adding and subtracting fractions with different denominators is a little more complicated.

First, you have to arrange the fractions so they have the same denominators.

The easiest way to do this is to multiply the denominators: For 2/5 + 1/2 multiply 5 by 2. Now you have a denominator of 10.

But now you have to change the top numbers too. Since you multiplied the 5 in 2/5 by 2, you also multiply the 2 by 2, to get 4. So the first fraction is now 4/10.

In the second fraction, you multiplied the denominator by 5, you have to multiply the numerator by 5 also, to get 5/10.

Now you have 4/10 + 5/10 and you can add 5 and 4 to get 9/10.

Simplest Form

To reduce a fraction to its simplest form, you have to arrange the numerator and denominator so the only common factor is 1.

Fractions, Decimals and Percent

Think of it this way:

Let's take an example: The fraction 2/10.

This is not reduced to its simplest terms because there is a number that will divide evenly into both: 2. We want to make it so that the only number that will divide evenly into both is 1.

Divide the top and bottom by 2 to get the new, reduced fraction - 1/5.

Multiplying Fractions

This is the easiest of all: Just multiply the two top numbers and then multiply the two bottom numbers.

Here is an example,

2/5 X 2/3

First, multiply the numerators: 2 X 2 = 4

then multiply the denominators: 5 X 3 = 15

Your answer is 4/15.

Dividing Fractions

Dividing fractions is easy if you remember a simple trick - first turn the second fraction upside down - then multiply!

Here is an example:

7/8 X 1/2

Turn the second fraction upside down:

7/8 X 2/1

then multiply:

(7 X 2) / (8 X 1) = 14/8

Converting Fractions to Decimals

There are a couple of ways to convert fractions to decimals. The first, which is the fastest -- is to memorize some basic fraction facts.

1/100 is "one hundredth," expressed as a decimal, it's .01.

1/50 is "two hundredths," expressed as a decimal, it's .02.

1/25 is "one twenty-fifth" or "four hundredths," expressed as a decimal, it's .04.

1/20 is "one twentieth" or ""five hundredths," expressed as a decimal, it's .05.

1/10 is "one tenth," expressed as a decimal, it's .1.

1/8 is "one eighth," or "one hundred twenty-five thousandths," expressed as a decimal, it's .125.

1/5 is "one fifth," or "two tenths," expressed as a decimal, it's .2.

1/4 is "one fourth" or "twenty-five hundredths," expressed as a decimal, it's .25.

1/3 is "one third" or "thirty-three hundredths," expressed as a decimal, it's .33.

1/2 is "one half" or "five tenths," expressed as a decimal, it's .5.

3/4 is "three fourths," or "seventy-five hundredths," expressed as a decimal, it's .75.

Of course, if you're no good at memorization, another

Fractions, Decimals and Percent

good technique for converting a fraction to a decimal is to manipulate it so that the fraction's denominator is 10, 100, 1000, or some other power of 10.

Here's an example: We'll start with three quarters. What is the first number in the 4 "times table" that you can multiply and get a multiple of 10? Can you multiply 4 by something to get 10? No. Can you multiply it by something to get 100? Yes! 4 X 25 is 100.

So multiply the numerator by 25, which is 75 over 100

We know fractions are really a division problem, and we also know that dividing by 100, means we move the decimal 2 places to the left.

So, 75 over 100 = .75

Lets try another example - Convert one fifth to a decimal.

First find a power of 10 that 5 goes into evenly, which is 2.

Multiply the numerator and denominator by 2, which is

two tenths.

Dividing 2 by 10 means we move the decimal place 1 place to the left.

So 1/5 = 0.5

Converting Fractions to Percent

Here is a quick method to convert fraction to percent and a strategy for answering on a multiple choice test that will save you valuable exam time.

First, remember that a fraction is a division problem: you're dividing the bottom number into the top.

Taking an example, convert 2/3 into percent.

The first method is to multiple the numerator by 100 and divide. So,

(2 X 100) / 2 = 100/3 = 66.66

Add a % sign and you have the answer, 66.66%

If you're doing these conversions on a multiple-choice test, here's an idea that might be even easier and faster. Let's say you have a fraction of 1/8 and you're asked to convert to percent.

Since we know that "percent" means hundredths, ask yourself what number we can multiply 8 by to get 100. Since there is no number, ask what number gets us close to 100.

That number is 12: 8 X 12 = 96. So it gets us a little less than 100. Now, whatever you do to the denominator, you have to do to the numerator. Let's multiply 1 X 12 and we get 12. However, since 96 is a little less than 100, we know that our answer will be a little MORE than 12%.

Look at the choices and eliminate the obvious wrong choices. So if your possible answers on the multiple-choice test are these:

a) 8.5% b) 19% c)12.5% d) 25%

then we know the answer is c) 12.5%, because it's a little MORE than the 12 we got in our math problem above.

Here all the choices except choice C 12.5% can be eliminated.

Fractions, Decimals and Percent

You don't have to know the exact correct answer, just enough to estimate, then eliminate the obviously wrong answers.

This was an easy example to demonstrate the strategy, but don't be fooled! You probably won't get such an easy question on your exam. By estimating your answer quickly, then eliminating obviously incorrect choices immediately, you save precious exam time.

Decimal Tips, Tricks and Short-cuts

Converting Decimals to Fractions

Converting decimals to fractions is easy if you say it the right way! If you say "point one" or "point 25," you'll have trouble.

But if you say, "one tenth" and "twenty-five hundredths," then you have already solved it! That's because, if you know your fractions, you know that "one tenth" looks like this: 1/10. And "twenty-five hundredths" looks like this: 25/100.

Even if you have digits before the decimal, such as 3.4, learning how to say the word will help you with the conversion into a fraction. It's not "three point four," it's "three and four tenths." Knowing this, you know that the fraction which looks like "three and four tenths" is 3 4/10.

The conversion is not complete until you reduce the fraction to its lowest terms: It's not 25/100, but 1/4.

Converting Decimals to Percent

Changing a decimal to a percent is easy if you remember one thing: multiply by 100.

For example, if you start with .45, simply multiply it by 100 for 45. Then add the % sign to the end - 45%.

Think of it this way: take out the decimal point, add a percent sign on the opposite side. In other words, the decimal on the left is replaced by the % on the right.

It doesn't work quite that easily if the decimal is in the middle of the number. For example, 3.7. Here, take out the decimal in the middle and replace it with a 0 % at the end. So 3.7 converted to decimal is 370%.

Percent Tips, Tricks and Short-cuts

Percent problems are not nearly as scary as they appear, if you remember this neat trick:

Draw a cross as in:

Portion	Percent
Whole	100

In the upper left, write PORTION. In the bottom left write WHOLE. In the top right, write PERCENT and in the bottom right, write 100. Whatever your problem is, you will leave blank the unknown, and fill in the other four parts. For example, let's suppose your problem is: Find 10% of

Fractions, Decimals and Percent

50. Since we know the 10% part, we put 10 in the percent corner. Since the whole number in our problem is 50, we put that in the corner marked whole. You always put 100 underneath the percent, so we leave it as is, which leaves only the top left corner blank. This is where we'll put our answer. Now simply multiply the two corner numbers that are NOT 100. Here, it's 10 X 50. That gives us 500. Now divide this by the remaining corner, or 100, to get a final answer of 5. 5 is the number that goes in the upper-left corner, and is your final solution.

Another hint to remember: Percents are the same thing as hundredths in decimals. So .45 is the same as 45 hundredths or 45 percent.

Converting Percents to Decimals

Percents are just a type of decimal, so it should be no surprise that converting between the two is actually fairly simple. Here are a few tricks and Short-cuts to keep in mind:

- Remember that percent literally means "per 100" or "for every 100." So when you speak of 30% you're saying 30 for every 100 or the fraction 30/100. In basic math, you learned that fractions that have 10 or 100 as the denominator can easily be turned to a decimal. 30/100 is thirty hundredths, or expressed as a decimal, .30.
- Another way to look at it: To convert a percent to a decimal, simply divide the number by 100. So for instance, if the percent is 47%, divide 47 by 100. The result will be .47. Get rid of the % mark and you're done.
- Remember that the easiest way of dividing by 100 is by moving your decimal two spots to the left.

Converting Percents to Fractions

Converting percents to fractions is easy. After all, a percent is just a type of fraction; it tells you what part of 100 that you're talking about. Here are some simple ideas for making the conversion from a percent to a fraction:

- If the percent is a whole number -- say 34% -- then simply write a fraction with 100 as the denominator (the bottom number). Then put the percentage itself on top. So 34% becomes 34/100.
- Now reduce as you would reduce any percent. Here, by dividing 2 into 34 and 2 into 100, you get 17/50.
- If your percent is not a whole number -- say 3.4% --then convert it to a decimal expressed as hundredths. 3.4 is the same as 3.40 (or 3 and forty hundredths). Now ask yourself how you would express "three and forty hundredths" as a fraction. It would, of course, be 3 40/100. Reduce this and it becomes 3 2/5.

Answer Sheet

	A	B	C	D	E			A	B	C	D	E
1	○	○	○	○	○		21	○	○	○	○	○
2	○	○	○	○	○		22	○	○	○	○	○
3	○	○	○	○	○		23	○	○	○	○	○
4	○	○	○	○	○		24	○	○	○	○	○
5	○	○	○	○	○		25	○	○	○	○	○
6	○	○	○	○	○		26	○	○	○	○	○
7	○	○	○	○	○		27	○	○	○	○	○
8	○	○	○	○	○		28	○	○	○	○	○
9	○	○	○	○	○		29	○	○	○	○	○
10	○	○	○	○	○		30	○	○	○	○	○
11	○	○	○	○	○							
12	○	○	○	○	○							
13	○	○	○	○	○							
14	○	○	○	○	○							
15	○	○	○	○	○							
16	○	○	○	○	○							
17	○	○	○	○	○							
18	○	○	○	○	○							
19	○	○	○	○	○							
20	○	○	○	○	○							

Practice Questions

1. 2/3 + 5/12 =

    a. 9/17`
    b. 3/11
    c. 7/12
    d. 1 1/12

2. 3/5 + 7/10 =

    a. 1 1/10
    b. 7/10
    c. 1 3/10
    d. 1 1/12

3. 4/5 – 2/3 =

    a. 2/2
    b. 2/13
    c. 1
    d. 2/15

4. 13/16 – 1/4 =

    a. 1
    b. 12/12
    c. 9/16
    d. 7/16

Fractions, Decimals and Percent

5. 15/16 x 8/9 =

    a. 5/6

    b. 16/37

    c. 2/11

    d. 5/7

6. 3/4 x 5/11 =

    a. 2/15

    b. 15/44

    c. 3/19

    d. 15/44

7. 5/8 ÷ 2/3 =

    a. 15/16

    b. 10/24

    c. 5/12

    d. 1 2/5

8. 2/15 ÷ 4/5 =

    a. 6/65

    b. 6/75

    c. 5/12

    d. 1/6

9. In a class of 83 students, 72 are present. What percent of the students are absent? Provide answer up to two significant digits.

    a. 12%
    b. 13%
    c. 14%
    d. 15%

10. A woman spent 15% of her income on an item and ends with $120. What percentage of her income is left?

    a. 12%
    b. 85%
    c. 75%
    d. 95%

11. X% of 120 = 30. Solve for X.

    a. 15
    b. 12
    c. 4
    d. 25

12. Simplify 6 3/5 – 4 4/5

    a. 1 4/5
    b. 2 3/5
    c. 2 9/5
    d. 1 1/5

Fractions, Decimals and Percent

13. Express 25% as a fraction.

    a. 1/4

    b. 7/40

    c. 6/25

    d. 8/28

14. Express 125% as a decimal.

    a. .125

    b. 12.5

    c. 1.25

    d. 125

15. Express 24/56 as a reduced common fraction.

    a. 4/9

    b. 4/11

    c. 3/7

    d. 3/8

16. Express 71/1000 as a decimal.

    a. .71

    b. .0071

    c. .071

    d. 7.1

17. .4% of 36 is

    a. 1.44

    b. .144

    c. 14.4

    d. 144

18. Express 0.27 + 0.33 as a fraction.

    a. 3/6

    b. 4/7

    c. 3/5

    d. 2/7

19. 8 is what percent of 40?

    a. 10%

    b. 15%

    c. 20%

    d. 25%

20. 3.14 + 2.73 + 23.7 =

    a. 28.57

    b. 30.57

    c. 29.56

    d. 29.57

21. What is 1/3 of 3/4?

    a. 1/4

    b. 1/3

    c. 2/3

    d. 3/48

22. 15 is what percent of 200?

    a. 7.5%

    b. 15%

    c. 20%

    d. 17.50%

―――― Fractions, Decimals and Percent ――――

23. A boy has 5 red balls, 3 white balls and 2 yellow balls. What percent of the balls are yellow?

    a. 2%
    b. 8%
    c. 20%
    d. 12%

24. Add 10% of 300 to 50% of 20

    a. 50
    b. 40
    c. 60
    d. 45

25. Convert 75% to a fraction.

    a. 2/100
    b. 85/100
    c. 3/4
    d. 4/7

26. Multiply 3 by 25% of 40.

    a. 75
    b. 30
    c. 68
    d. 35

27. What is 10% of 30 multiplied by 75% of 200?

a. 450
b. 750
c. 20
d. 45

28. Convert 4/20 to percent.

a. 25%
b. 20%
c. 40%
d. 30%

29. Write 765.3682 to the nearest 1000th.

a. 765.368
b. 765.36
c. 765.3682
d. 765.3

30. What number is in the ten thousandths place in 1.7389?

a. 1
b. 8
c. 9
d. 3

Answer Key

1. D
A common denominator is needed, which both 3 and 12 will divide into. So, 8 + 5/12 = 13/12 = 1 1/12

2. C
A common denominator is needed for 5 and 10.
6 + 7/10 = 13/10 = 1 3/10

3. D
A common denominator is needed for 5 and 3.
12 - 10/15 = 2/15

4. C
A common denominator is needed for 16 and 4.
13 - 4/16 = 9/16

5. A
Since there are common numerators and denominators to cancel out, we cancel out 15/16 x 8/9 to get 5/2 x 1/3, and then multiply numerators and denominators to get 5/6

6. D
Since there are no common numerators and denominators to cancel out, we simply multiply the numerators and then the denominators. So 3 x 5/4 x 11 = 15/44

7. A
To divide fractions, multiply the first fraction with the inverse of the second. 5/8 x 3/2, = 15/16

8. D
Multiply the first fraction with the inverse of the second.
2/15 x 5/4, (cancel out) = 1/3 x 1/2 = 1/6

9. B
Number of absent students = 83 – 72 = 11

Percentage of absent students is found by proportioning the number of absent students to the total number of students in the class = 11 * 100/83 = 13.25

Checking the answer, round 13.25 to the nearest whole number: 13%.

10. B
Spent 15%, so 100% - 15% = 85%

11. D
X% of 120 = 30,
X/100 = 30/120
So X = 30/120 x 100/1
3000/120 = 300/12
X = 25

12. A
(6-4) (3/5 – 4/5) = 2 (3-4/5) = since 3 is less than 4, we would have to subtract 1 from the whole number besides the fraction, therefore 1 4/5

13. A
25% = 25/100 = 1/4

14. C
125/100 = 1.25

15. C
24/56 = 3/7 (divide numerator and denominator by 8)

16. C
Converting a fraction into a decimal – divide the numerator by the denominator – so 71/1000 = .071. Dividing by 1000 moves the decimal point 3 places to the left.

Fractions, Decimals and Percent

17. B
.4/100 * 36 = .4 * 36/100 = .144

18. C
To convert a decimal to a fraction, take the places of decimal as your denominator, here, 2, so in 0.27, '7' is in the 100th place, so the fraction is 27/100 and 0.33 becomes 33/100.

Next estimate the answer quickly to eliminate obvious wrong choices. 27/100 is about 1/4 and 33/100 is 1/3. 1/3 is slightly larger than 1/4, and 1/4 + 1/4 is 1/2, so the answer will be slightly larger than 1/2.
Looking at the choices, Choice A can be eliminated since 3/6 = 1/2. Choice D, 2/7 is less than 1/2 and be eliminated. The answer is going to be Choice B or Choice C.

Do the calculation, 0.27 + 0.33 = 0.60 and 0.60 = 60/100 = 3/5, Choice C is correct.

19. C
This is an easy question, and shows how you can solve some questions without doing the calculations. The question is, 8 is what percent of 40. Take easy percentages for an approximate answer and see what you get.

10% is easy to calculate because you can drop the zero, or move the decimal point. 10% of 40 = 4, and 8 = 2 X 4, so, 8 must be 2 X 10% = 20%.

Here are the calculations which confirm the quick approximation.
8/40 = X/100 = 8 * 100 / 40X = 800/40 = X = 20

20. D
3.14 + 2.73 = 5.87 and 5.87 + 23.7 = 29.57

21. A
1/3 X 3/4 = 3/12 = 1/4
To multiply fractions, multiply the numerator and denominator.

22. A
15/200 = X/100
200X = (15 * 100)
1500/200 Cancel zeros in the numerator and denominator 15/2 = 7.5%.

Notice that the questions asks, What 15 is what percent of 200? The question does *not* ask, what is 15% of 200! The answers are very different.

23. C
Total no. of balls = 10, no. of yellow balls = 2, answer = 2/10 X 100 = 20%.

24. B
10% of 300 = 30 and 50% of 20 = 10 so 30 + 10 = 40.

25. C
75% = 75/100 = 3/4

26. B
25% of 40 = 10 and 10 x 3 = 30

27. A
10% of 30 = 3 and 75% of 200 = 150, 3 X 150 = 450

28. B
4/20 X 100 = 1/5 X 100 = 20%

29. A
The number is 51.738. The last digit, in the 1,000th place, 2, is less than 5, so it is discarded. Answer = 765.368.

Fractions, Decimals and Percent

30. C
9 is in the ten thousandths place in 1.7389, which is 4 places to the right of the decimal point.

Metric Conversion

Conversion between metric and standard units can be tricky since the units of distance, volume, area and temperature can seem arbitrary when compared. Although the metric system (using SI units) is the standard system of measure in most parts of the world many countries still use at least some of their traditional units of measure. In North America those units come from the old British system.

When measuring distance the relation between metric and standard units looks like this:

0.039 in	1 millimeter	1 inch	25.4 mm
3.28 ft	1 meter	1 foot	.305 m
0.621 mi	1 kilometer	1 mile	1.61 km

Here, you can see that 1 millimeter is equal to .039 inches and 1 inch equals 25.4 millimeters.

When measuring area the relation between metric and standard looks like this:

Metric Conversion

.0016 in²	1 millimeter²	1 inch²	645.2 mm²
10.764 ft²	1 meter²	1 foot²	.093 m²
.386 mi²	1 kilometer²	1 mile²	2.59 km²
2.47 ac	hectare	1 acre	.405 ha

Similarly, when measuring volume the relation between metric and standard units looks like this:

3034 fl oz	1 milliliter	1 fluid ounce	29.57 ml
.0264 gal	1 liter	1 gallon	3.785 L
35.314 ft³	1 cubic meter	1 cubic foot	.028 m³

When measuring weight and mass the relation between metric and standard units looks like this:

.035 oz	1 gram	1 ounce	28.35 g
2.202 lbs	1 kilogram	1 pound	.454 kg
1.103 T	1 metric ton	1 ton	.907 t

Note that in science, the metric units of grams and kilograms are always used to denote the mass of an object rather than its weight.

In predominantly metric countries the standard unit of temperature is degrees Celsius while in countries with only limited use of the metric system, such as the United States, degrees Fahrenheit is used. This chart shows the difference between Fahrenheit and Celsius:

Celsius	Fahrenheit
0° Celsius	32° Fahrenheit
10° Celsius	50° Fahrenheit
20° Celsius	68° Fahrenheit
30° Celsius	86° Fahrenheit
40° Celsius	104° Fahrenheit
50° Celsius	122° Fahrenheit
60° Celsius	140° Fahrenheit
70° Celsius	158° Fahrenheit
80° Celsius	176° Fahrenheit
90° Celsius	194° Fahrenheit
100° Celsius	212° Fahrenheit

As you can see 0° C is freezing while 32° F is freezing. Similarity 100° C is boiling while the Fahrenheit system takes until 212° F. To convert from Celsius to Fahrenheit you need to multiply the temperature in Celsius by 1.8 and then add 32 to it. (x° F = (y° C*1.8) + 32) To convert from Fahrenheit to Celsius you do the opposite. First subtract 32 from the temperature then divide by 1.8. (x° C = (y° -32) / 1.8)

Answer Sheet

	A	B	C	D
1	○	○	○	○
2	○	○	○	○
3	○	○	○	○
4	○	○	○	○
5	○	○	○	○
6	○	○	○	○
7	○	○	○	○
8	○	○	○	○
9	○	○	○	○
10	○	○	○	○
11	○	○	○	○
12	○	○	○	○
13	○	○	○	○
14	○	○	○	○
15	○	○	○	○

1. Convert 10 kg. to grams.

    10,000 grams
    1,000 grams
    100 grams
    10.11 grams

2. 1 gallon = _____ liter(s).

    a. 1 liter
    b. 3.785 liters
    c. 37.85 liters
    d. 4.5 liters

3. Convert 2.5 liters to milliliters.

    a. 1,050 ml.
    b. 2,500 ml.
    c. 2,050 ml.
    d. 1,500 ml.

4. Convert 210 mg. to grams.

    a. 0.21 mg.
    b. 2.1 g.
    c. 0.21 g.
    d. 2.12 g.

5. Convert 10 pounds to kilograms.

    a. 4.54 kg.
    b. 11.25 kg.
    c. 15 kg.
    d. 10.25 kg.

Metric Conversion

6. Convert 0.539 grams to milligrams.

   a. 539 g.
   b. 539 mg.
   c. 53.9 mg.
   d. 0.53 g.

7. Convert 16 quarts to gallons.

   a. 1 gallons
   b. 8 gallons
   c. 4 gallons
   d. 4.5 gallons

8. Convert 45 kg. to pounds.

   a. 10 pounds
   b. 100 pounds
   c. 1,000 pounds
   d. 110 pounds

9. Convert 60 feet to inches.

   a. 700 inches
   b. 600 inches
   c. 720 inches
   d. 1,800 inches

10. Convert 100 millimeters to centimeters.

   a. 10 centimeters
   b. 1,000 centimeters
   c. 1100 centimeters
   d. 50 centimeters

11. Convert 3 gallons to quarts.

    a. 15 quarts
    b. 6 quarts
    c. 12 quarts
    d. 32 quarts

12. 0.05 ml. =

    a. 50 liters
    b. 0.00005 liters
    c. 5 liters
    d. 0.0005 liters

13. Convert .45 meters to centimeters

    a. 45
    b. 450
    c. 4.5
    d. .45

14. Convert 0.007 kilograms to grams

    a. 7g
    b. 70g
    c. 0.07g
    d. 0.70g

15. Convert 0.63g to mg.

    a. 630g
    b. 63mg
    c. 630 mg
    d. 603mg

Answer Key

1. A
1 kg = 1,000 g and 10 kg = 10 x 1,000 = 10,000 g

2. B
1 US gallon = 3.78541178 liters

3. B
1 liter = 1,000 milliliters, 2.5 liters = 2.5 x 1,000 = 2,500 milliliters

4. C
1,000 mg = 1 g, 210 mg = 210/1000 = 0.21 g. Be careful of Choice A, (0.21 mg.) The numbers are the same but the units are different.

5. A
1 pound = 0.45 kg, 10 pounds = 4.53592, or about 4.54 kg. When multiplying a decimal by 10, move the decimal point one place to the left.

6. B
1 g = 1,000 mg. 0.539 g = 0.539 x 1000 = 539 mg.

7. C
4 quarts = 1 gallon, 16 quarts = 16/4 = 4 gallons. Conversion problems are easy to get confused. One way to think of them is which is larger - quarts or gallons? Gallons are larger, so if you are converting from quarts to gallons the number of gallons will be a smaller number. Keeping that in mind, do a 'common-sense' check on the answer.

8. B
0.45 kg = 1 pound, 1 kg. = 1/0.45 and 45 kg = 1/0.45 x 45 = 99.208, or 100 pounds.

9. C
1 foot = 12 inches, 60 feet = 60 x 12 = 720 inches.

10. A
1 millimeter = 10 centimeter, 100 millimeter = 100/10 = 10 centimeters.

11. C
1 gallon = 4 quarts, 3 gallons = 3 x 4 = 12 quarts.

12. B
There are 1000 ml in a liter. 0.05/1000 = 0.00005 liters.

13. A
There are 100 centimeters in a meter, so 100 X .45 meters = 45 centimeters.

14. A
1000g = lg., 0.007 = 1000 x 0.007 = 7g.

15. C
1 g = 1,000 mg. 0.63g = 0.63 x 1,000 = 630mg.

Basic Algebra

The Basic Algebra section covers the following:

- Ratio and proportion
- Linear equations with 1 variables
- Quadratics
- Operations with polynomials

Solving One-Variable Linear Equations

Linear equations with variable x is an equation with the following form:
$$ax = b$$

where a and b are real numbers. If a=0 and b is different from 0, then the equation has no solution.

Let's solve one simple example of a linear equation with one variable:
$$4x - 2 = 2x + 6$$

When given this type of equation, move variables to one side, and real numbers to the other. Always remember: if you are changing sides, you are changing signs. Move all variables to the left, and real numbers to the right:

$4x - 2 = 2x + 6$
$4x - 2x = 6 + 2$
$2x = 8$
$x = 8/2$
$x = 4$

When 2x goes to the left it becomes -2x, and -2 goes to the right and becomes +2. After calculations, we find that x is 4, which is a solution of our linear equation.

Let's solve a little more complex linear equation:

2x - 6/4 + 4 = x
2x - 6 + 16 = 4x
2x - 4x = -16 + 6
-2x = -10
x = -10/-2
x = 5

We multiply whole equation by 4, to lose the fractional line. Now we have a simple linear equation. If we change sides, we change the signs.

Simplifying Polynomials

Let's say we are given some expression with one or more variables, where we have to add, subtract and multiply polynomials. We do the calculations with variables and constants and then we group the variables with the appropriate degrees. As a result, we would get a polynomial. This process is called simplifying polynomials, where we go from a complex expression to a simple polynomial.

Example:

Simplify the following expression and arrange the degrees from bigger to smaller:

$4 + 3x - 2x^2 + 5x + 6x^3 - 2x^2 + 1 = 6x^3 - 4x^2 + 8x + 5$

We can have more complex expressions such as:

$(x + 5)(1 - x) - (2x - 2) = x - x^2 + 5 - 5x - 2x + 2 = -x^2 - 6x + 7$

Here, first we multiply the polynomials and then we subtract the result and the third polynomial.

Factoring Polynomials

If we have a polynomial that we want to write as multiplication of a real number and a polynomial or as a multiplication of 2 or more polynomials, then we are dealing with factoring polynomials.

Let's see an example for a simple factoring:

$12x^2 + 6x - 4 =$
$2 * 6x^2 + 2 * 3x - 2 * 2 =$
$2(6x^2 + 3x - 2)$

We look at every polynomial member as a product of a real number and a variable. Notice that all real numbers in the polynomial are even, so they have the same number (factor). We pull out that 2 in front of the polynomial, and we write what is left.

What if have a more complex case, where we can't find a factor that is a real number? Here is an example:

$x^2 - 2x + 1 =$
$x^2 - x - x + 1 =$
$x(x - 1) - (x - 1) =$
$(x - 1)(x - 1)$

We can write -2x as –x-x . Now we group first 2 members and we see that they have the same factor x, which we can pull in front of them. For the other 2 members, we pull the minus in front of them, so we can get the same binomial that we got with the first 2 members. Now we have that this binomial is the factor for x(x-1) and (x-1).

If we pull x-1 in front (underlined), from the first member we are left with x, and from the second we have -1.
And that is how we transform a polynomial into a product of 2 polynomials (in this case binomials).

Quadratic Equations

A. Factoring

Quadratic equations are usually called second degree equations, which mean that the second degree is the highest degree of the variable that can be found in the quadratic equation. The form of these equations is:

$ax^2 + bx + c = 0$

where a, b and c are some real numbers.

One way for solving quadratic equations is the factoring method, where we transform the quadratic equation into a product of 2 or more polynomials. Let's see how that works in one simple example:

x2 + 2x = 0
x(x + 2) = 0
(x = 0) V (x + 2 = 0)
(x = 0 V (x + -2)

Notice that here we don't have parameter c, but this is still a quadratic equation, because we have the second degree of variable x. Our factor here is x, which we put in front, and we are left with x+2. The equation is equal to 0, so either x or x+2 are 0, or both are 0.
So, our 2 solutions are 0 and -2.

B. Quadratic formula

If we are unsure how to rewrite quadratic equations so we can solve it using factoring method, we can use the formula for quadratic equation:

$$x_{1,2} = \frac{-b \pm \sqrt{b^2 - 4ac}}{2a}$$

We write $x_{1,2}$ because it represents 2 solutions of the equation. Here is one example:

$$3x^2 - 10x + 3 = 0$$

$$x_{1,2} = \frac{-b \pm \sqrt{b^2 - 4ac}}{2a}$$

$$x_{1,2} = \frac{-(-10) \pm \sqrt{(-10)^2 - 4 \cdot 3 \cdot 3}}{2 \cdot 3}$$

$$x_{1,2} = \frac{10 \pm \sqrt{100 - 36}}{6}$$

$$x_{1,2} = \frac{10 \pm \sqrt{64}}{6}$$

$$x_{1,2} = \frac{10 \pm 8}{6}$$

$$x_1 = \frac{10 + 8}{6} = \frac{18}{6} = 3$$

$$x_2 = \frac{10 - 8}{6} = \frac{2}{6} = \frac{1}{3}$$

We see that a is 3, b is -10 and c is 3.
We use these numbers in the equation and do some calculations.

Notice that we have + and -, so x_1 is for + and x_2 is for -, and that's how we get 2 solutions.

Answer Sheet

	A	B	C	D	E		A	B	C	D	E
1	○	○	○	○	○	21	○	○	○	○	○
2	○	○	○	○	○	22	○	○	○	○	○
3	○	○	○	○	○	23	○	○	○	○	○
4	○	○	○	○	○	24	○	○	○	○	○
5	○	○	○	○	○	25	○	○	○	○	○
6	○	○	○	○	○	26	○	○	○	○	○
7	○	○	○	○	○	27	○	○	○	○	○
8	○	○	○	○	○	28	○	○	○	○	○
9	○	○	○	○	○	29	○	○	○	○	○
10	○	○	○	○	○	30	○	○	○	○	○
11	○	○	○	○	○						
12	○	○	○	○	○						
13	○	○	○	○	○						
14	○	○	○	○	○						
15	○	○	○	○	○						
16	○	○	○	○	○						
17	○	○	○	○	○						
18	○	○	○	○	○						
19	○	○	○	○	○						
20	○	○	○	○	○						

Basic Algebra Practice

1. Solve the linear equation: -x - 7 = -3x - 9

    a. -1
    b. 0
    c. 1
    d. 2

2. Solve the system: 4x - y = 5   x + 2y = 8

    a. (3,2)
    b. (3,3)
    c. (2,3)
    d. (2,2)

3. Simplify the following expression:

$3x^3 + 2x^2 + 5x - 7 + 4x^2 - 5x + 2 - 3x^3$

    a. $6x^2 - 9$
    b. $6x^2 - 5$
    c. $6x^2 - 10x - 5$
    d. $6x^2 + 10x - 9$

4. Using the factoring method, solve the quadratic equation: $x^2 + 4x + 4 = 0$

    a. 0 and 1
    b. 1 and 2
    c. 2
    d. -2

5. Using the quadratic formula, solve the quadratic equation: $x - 31/x = 0$

    a. $-\sqrt{13}$ and $\sqrt{13}$
    b. $-\sqrt{31}$ and $\sqrt{31}$
    c. $-\sqrt{31}$ and $2\sqrt{31}$
    d. $-\sqrt{3}$ and $\sqrt{3}$

6. Using the factoring method, solve the quadratic equation: $2x^2 - 3x = 0$

    a. 0 and 1.5
    b. 1.5 and 2
    c. 2 and 2.5
    d. 0 and 2

7. Using the quadratic formula, solve the quadratic equation: $x^2 - 9x + 14 = 0$

    a. 2 and 7
    b. -2 and 7
    c. -7 and -2
    d. -7 and 2

8. Solve the following equation $4(y + 6) = 3y + 30$

    a. $y = 20$
    b. $y = 6$
    c. $y = 30/7$
    d. $y = 30$

Basic Algebra

9. Using the factoring method, solve the quadratic equation: $x^2 - 5x - 6 = 0$

    a. -6 and 1

    b. -1 and 6

    c. 1 and 6

    d. -6 and -1

10. Factor the polynomial $x^3y^3 - x^2y^8$.

    a. $x^2y^3(x - y^5)$

    b. $x^3y^3(1 - y^5)$

    c. $x^2y^2(x - y^6)$

    d. $xy^3(x - y^5)$

11. Find the solution for the following linear equation: $5x/2 = (3x + 24)/6$

    a. -1

    b. 0

    c. 1

    d. 2

12. Solve $3(x + 2) - 2(1 - x) = 4x + 5$

    a. -1

    b. 0

    c. 1

    d. 2

13. Simplify $3x^a + 6a^x - x^a + (-5a^x) - 2x^a$

   a. $a^x + x^a$
   b. $a^x - x^a$
   c. a^x
   d. x^a

14. A map uses a scale of 1:100,000. How much distance on the ground is 3 inches on the map if the scale is in inches?

   a. 13 inches
   b. 300,000 inches
   c. 30,000 inches
   d. 333.999 inches

15. Using the quadratic formula, solve the quadratic equation: $0.9x^2 + 1.8x - 2.7 = 0$

   a. 1 and 3
   b. -3 and 1
   c. -3 and -1
   d. -1 and 3

16. Using the factoring method, solve the quadratic equation: $x^2 + 12x - 13 = 0$

   a. -13 and 1
   b. -13 and -1
   c. 1 and 13
   d. -1 and 13

Basic Algebra

17. Using the quadratic formula, solve the quadratic equation: $((x^2 + 4x + 4) + (x^2 - 4x + 4)) / (x^2 - 4) = 0$.

    a. It has infinite numbers of solutions

    b. 0 and 1

    c. It has no solutions

    d. 0

18. Turn the following expression into a simple polynomial: $5(3x^2 - 2) - x^2(2 - 3x)$

    a. $3x^3 + 17x^2 - 10$

    b. $3x^3 + 13x^2 + 10$

    c. $-3x^3 - 13x^2 - 10$

    d. $3x^3 + 13x^2 - 10$

19. Solve $(x^3 + 2)(x^2 - x) - x^5$.

    a. $2x^5 - x^4 + 2x^2 - 2x$

    b. $-x^4 + 2x^2 - 2x$

    c. $-x^4 - 2x^2 - 2x$

    d. $-x^4 + 2x^2 + 2x$

20. Factor the polynomial $x^2 - 7x - 30$.

    a. $(x + 15)(x - 2)$

    b. $(x + 10)(x - 3)$

    c. $(x - 10)(x + 3)$

    d. $(x - 15)(x + 2)$

21. If a and b are real numbers, solve the following equation: $(a + 2)x - b = -2 + (a + b)x$

   a. -1
   b. 0
   c. 1
   d. 2

22. Turn the following expression into a simple polynomial: $1 - x(1 - x(1 - x))$

   a. $x^3 + x^2 - x + 1$
   b. $-x^3 - x^2 + x + 1$
   c. $-x^3 + x^2 - x + 1$
   d. $x^3 + x^2 - x - 1$

23. $7(2y + 8) + 1 - 4(y + 5) =$

   a. $10y + 36$
   b. $10y + 77$
   c. $18y + 37$
   d. $10y + 37$

24. Richard gives 's' amount of salary to each of his 'n' employees weekly. If he has 'x' amount of money then how many days he can employ these 'n' employees.

   a. sx/7n
   b. 7x/nx
   c. nx/7s
   d. 7x/ns

25. Factor the polynomial $x^2 - 3x - 4$.

   a. $(x + 1)(x - 4)$
   b. $(x - 1)(x + 4)$
   c. $(x - 1)(x - 4)$
   d. $(x + 1)(x + 4)$

26. Using the quadratic formula, solve the quadratic equation:

$(a^2 - b^2)x^2 + 2ax + 1 = 0$

   a. $a/(a + b)$ and $b/(a + b)$
   b. $1/(a + b)$ and $a/(a + b)$
   c. $a/(a + b)$ and $a/(a - b)$
   d. $-1/(a + b)$ and $-1/(a - b)$

27. Turn the following expression into a simple polynomial: $(a + b)(x + y) + (a - b)(x - y) - (ax + by)$

   a. $ax + by$
   b. $ax - by$
   c. $ax^2 + by^2$
   d. $ax^2 - by^2$

28. A number is increased by 2 and then multiplied by 3. The result is 24. What is this number?

   a. 4
   b. 6
   c. 8
   d. 10

29. My father's age divided by 5 is equal to my brother's age divided by 3. My brother is 3 years older than me. My father's age is 3 less than 2 times my age. How old is my father?

    a. 34
    b. 45
    c. 56
    d. 61

30. $(x - 2)/4 - (3x + 5)/7 = -3$, $x=?$

    a. 6
    b. 7
    c. 10
    d. 13

Answer Key

1. A

We should collect similar terms on the same side. Here, we can collect x terms on left side, and the constants on the right side:

- x - 7 = - 3x - 9 .... Let us add 3x to both sides:

- x - 7 + 3x = - 3x - 9 + 3x

2x - 7 = - 9 ... Now, we can add + 7 to both sides:

2x - 7 + 7 = - 9 + 7

2x = - 2 ... Dividing both sides by 2 gives us the value of x:

x = -2/2

x = -1

2. C

First, we need to write two equations separately:
4x - y = 5 (I)

x + 2y = 8 (II) ... Here, we can use two ways to solve the system. One is substitution method, the other one is linear elimination method:

1. Substitution Method

Equation (I) gives us that y = 4x - 5. We insert this value of y into equation (II):

x + 2(4x - 5) = 8

x + 8x - 10 = 8

9x - 10 = 8

$9x = 18$

$x = 2$

Bu knowing x = 2, we can find the value of y by inserting x = 2 into either of the equations. Let us choose equation (I):

$4(2) - y = 5$

$8 - y = 5$

$8 - 5 = y$

$y = 3 \rightarrow$ solution is (2, 3)

2. Linear Elimination Method:

2 * / 4x - y = 5 ... by multiplying equation (I) by 2, we see that -2y will form; and y terms

    x + 2y = 8 ... will be eliminated when summed with +2y in equation (II):

2 * / 4x - y = 5

+   <u>x + 2y = 8</u>

    8x - 2y = 10

+ <u>x + 2y = 8</u> ... Summing side by side:

8x + x - 2y + 2y = 10 + 8 ... -2y and +2y eliminate each other:

$9x = 18$

$x = 2$

By knowing x = 2, we can find the value of y by inserting x = 2 into either of the equations. Let us choose equation (I):

Basic Algebra

$4(2) - y = 5$

$8 - y = 5$

$8 - 5 = y$

$y = 3 \rightarrow$ solution is (2, 3)

3. B
$3x^3 + 2x^2 + 5x - 7 + 4x^2 - 5x + 2 - 3x^3$ ... write similar terms together:

$= 3x^3 - 3x^3 + 2x^2 + 4x^2 + 5x - 5x - 7 + 2$ ... operate within the same terms. $3x^3$ and $-3x^3$, $5x$ and $-5x$ cancel:

$= 6x^2 - 5$

4. D
$x^2 + 4x + 4 = 0$ ... We try to separate the middle term $4x$ to find common factors with $x2$ and 4 separately:

$x^2 + 2x + 2x + 4 = 0$ ... Here, we see that x is a common factor for x^2 and $2x$, and 2 is a common factor for $2x$ and 4:

$x(x + 2) + 2(x + 2) = 0$ ... Here, we have x times x + 2 and 2 times x + 2 summed up. This means that we have x + 2 times x + 2:

$(x + 2)(x + 2) = 0$

$(x + 2)^2 = 0$ ... This is true if only if x + 2 is equal to zero.

$x + 2 = 0$

$x = -2$

5. B
To solve the equation, first we need to arrange it to appear in the form $ax^2 + bx + c = 0$ by removing the denominator:

$x - 31/x = 0$ ... First, we enlarge the equation by x:

$x * x - 31 * x/x = 0$

$x^2 - 31 = 0$

The quadratic formula to find the roots of a quadratic equation is:

$x_{1,2} = (-b \pm \sqrt{\Delta}) / 2a$ where $\Delta = b^2 - 4ac$ and is called the discriminant of the quadratic equation.

In our question, the equation is $x^2 - 31 = 0$. By remembering the form $ax^2 + bx + c = 0$:

$a = 1, b = 0, c = -31$

So, we can find the discriminant first, and then the roots of the equation:

$\Delta = b^2 - 4ac = 0^2 - 4 * 1 * (-31) = 124$

$x_{1,2} = (-b \pm \sqrt{\Delta}) / 2a = (\pm\sqrt{124}) / 2 = (\pm\sqrt{4 * 31}) / 2 = (\pm 2\sqrt{31}) / 2$ ... Simplifying by 2:

$x_{1,2} = \pm\sqrt{31}$ ... This means that the roots are $\sqrt{31}$ and $-\sqrt{31}$.

6. A

$2x^2 - 3x = 0$ ... we see that both of the terms contain x; so we can take it out as a factor:

$x(2x - 3) = 0$ ... two terms are multiplied and the result is zero. This means that either of the terms or, both can be equal to zero:

$x = 0$ ... this is one solution

$2x - 3 = 0 \rightarrow 2x = 3 \rightarrow x = 3/2 \rightarrow x = 1.5$ ... this is the second solution.

So, the solutions are 0 and 1.5.

7. A

To solve the equation, we need the equation in the form $ax^2 + bx + c = 0$.

$x^2 - 9x + 14 = 0$ is already in this form.

The quadratic formula to find the roots of a quadratic equation is:

$x_{1,2} = (-b \pm \sqrt{\Delta}) / 2a$ where $\Delta = b^2 - 4ac$ and is called the discriminant of the quadratic equation.

In our question, the equation is $x^2 - 9x + 14 = 0$. By remembering the form $ax^2 + bx + c = 0$:

$a = 1, b = -9, c = 14$

So, we can find the discriminant first, and then the roots of the equation:

$\Delta = b^2 - 4ac = (-9)^2 - 4 * 1 * 14 = 81 - 56 = 25$

$x_{1,2} = (-b \pm \sqrt{\Delta}) / 2a = (-(-9) \pm \sqrt{25}) / 2 = (9 \pm 5) / 2$

This means that the roots are,

$x_1 = (9 - 5) / 2 = 2$ and $x_2 = (9 + 5) / 2 = 7$

8. B
$4y + 24 = 3y + 30, = 4y - 3y + 24 = 30, = y + 24 = 30, = y = 30 - 24, = y = 6$

9. B
$x^2 - 5x - 6 = 0$

We try to separate the middle term $-5x$ to find common factors with x^2 and -6 separately:

$x^2 - 6x + x - 6 = 0$ ... Here, we see that x is a common factor for x^2 and $-6x$:

$x(x - 6) + x - 6 = 0$ ... Here, we have x times x - 6 and 1 time x - 6 summed up. This means that we have x + 1 times x - 6:

$(x + 1)(x - 6) = 0$ ... This is true when either or both of the expressions in the parenthesis are equal to zero:

$x + 1 = 0$ ... $x = -1$

$x - 6 = 0$ ... $x = 6$

-1 and 6 are the solutions for this quadratic equation.

10. A
We need to find the greatest common divisor of the two terms to factor the expression. We should remember that if the bases of exponent numbers are the same, the multiplication of two terms is found by summing the powers and writing on the same base. Similarly; when dividing, the power of the divisor is subtracted from the power of the divided.

Both x^3y^3 and x^2y^8 contain x^2 and y^3. So;

$x^3y^3 - x^2y^8 = x * x^2y^3 - y^5 * x^2y^3$ ... We can carry x^2y^3 out as the factor:

$= x^2y^3(x - y^5)$

11. D
Our aim to collect the knowns on one side and the unknowns (x terms) on the other side:

$5x/2 = (3x + 24)/6$ ... First, we can simplify the denominators of both sides by 2:

$5x = (3x + 24)/3$ ... Now, we can cross multiply:

$15x = 3x + 24$

15x - 3x = 24

12x = 24

x = 24/12 = 2

12. C
To solve the linear equation, we operate the knowns and unknowns within each other and try to obtain x term (which is the unknown) alone on one side of the equation: 3(x + 2) - 2(1 - x) = 4x + 5 ... We remove the parenthesis by distributing the factors:

3x + 6 - 2 + 2x = 4x + 5

5x + 4 = 4x + 5

5x - 4x = 5 - 4

x = 1

13. C
Here, we use the commutative property of multiplication, meaning that xa = ax:
3xa + 6ax - xa + (-5ax) - 2xa = 3ax + 6ax - ax - 5ax - 2ax
= (3 + 6 - 1 - 5 - 2)ax
= (9 - 8)ax
= ax

14. B
1 inch on map = 100,000 inches on ground. So 3 inches on map = 3 x 100,000 = 300,000 inches on ground.

15. B
To solve the equation, we need the equation in the form $ax^2 + bx + c = 0$.

$0.9x^2 + 1.8x - 2.7 = 0$ is already in this form.
The quadratic formula to find the roots of a quadratic equation is:

$x_{1,2} = (-b \pm \sqrt{\Delta}) / 2a$ where $\Delta = b^2 - 4ac$ and is called the discriminant of the quadratic equation.

In our question, the equation is $0.9x^2 + 1.8x - 2.7 = 0$. To eliminate the decimals, let us multiply the equation by 10: $9x^2 + 18x - 27 = 0$ ... This equation can be simplified by 9 since each term contains 9:

$x^2 + 2x - 3 = 0$

By remembering the form $ax^2 + bx + c = 0$:

$a = 1, b = 2, c = -3$

So, we can find the discriminant first, and then the roots of the equation:

$\Delta = b^2 - 4ac = (2)^2 - 4 * 1 * (-3) = 4 + 12 = 16$

$x_{1,2} = (-b \pm \sqrt{\Delta}) / 2a = (-2 \pm \sqrt{16}) / 2 = (-2 \pm 4) / 2$

This means that the roots are,

$x_1 = (-2 - 4)/2 = -3$ and $x_2 = (-2 + 4)/2 = 1$

16. A
$x^2 + 12x - 13 = 0$ ... We try to separate the middle term $12x$ to find common factors with x^2 and -13 separately:

$x^2 + 13x - x - 13 = 0$ ... Here, we see that x is a common factor for x^2 and $13x$, and -1 is a common factor for $-x$ and -13:

$x(x + 13) - 1(x + 13) = 0$ ... Here, we have x times $x + 13$ and -1 times $x + 13$ summed up. This means that we have $x - 1$ times $x + 13$:

$(x - 1)(x + 13) = 0$

This is true when either, or both, the expressions in the parenthesis are equal to zero:

x - 1 = 0 ... x = 1

x + 13 = 0 ... x = -13

1 and -13 are the solutions for this quadratic equation.

17. C
First, we need to simplify the equation:
$((x^2 + 4x + 4) + (x^2 - 4x + 4)) / (x^2 - 4) = 0$

$(x^2 + 4x + 4 + x^2 - 4x + 4) / (x^2 - 4) = 0$ ... 4x and -4x in the numerator cancel.

Note that $x^2 - 4$ is two square difference and is equal to $x^2 - 2^2 = (x - 2)(x + 2)$:

$(2x^2 + 8)/((x - 2)(x + 2)) = 0$

The denominator tells us that if x - 2 or x + 2 equals to zero, there will be no solution. So, we will need to eliminate x = 2 and x = -2 from our solution which will be found considering the numerator:

$2x^2 + 8 = 0$

$2(x^2 + 4) = 0$

$x^2 + 4 = 0$

$x^2 = -4$ ... We know that, a square cannot be equal to a negative number. Solution for the square root of -4 is not a real number, so this equation has no solution.

18. D
We need to distribute the factors to the terms inside the related parenthesis:

$5(3x^2 - 2) - x^2(2 - 3x) = 15x^2 - 10 - (2x^2 - 3x^3)$

$= 15x^2 - 10 - 2x^2 + 3x^3$

$= 3x^3 + 15x^2 - 2x^2 - 10$ ... similar terms written together to ease summing/substituting.

$= 3x^3 + 13x^2 - 10$

19. B
We need to distribute the factors to the terms inside the related parenthesis:

$(x^3 + 2)(x^2 - x) - x^5 = x^5 - x^4 + (2x^2 - 2x) - x^5$

$= x^5 - x^4 + 2x^2 - 2x - x^5$

$= x^5 - x^5 - x^4 + 2x^2 - 2x$ ... similar terms written together to ease summing/substituting.

$= -x^4 + 2x^2 - 2x$

20. C
$x^2 - 7x - 30 = 0$ ... We try to separate the middle term $-7x$ to find common factors with x^2 and -30 separately:

$x^2 - 10x + 3x - 30 = 0$ ... Here, we see that x is a common factor for x^2 and $-10x$, and 3 is a common factor for $3x$ and -30:

$x(x - 10) + 3(x - 10) = 0$ ... Here, we have x times $x - 10$ and 3 times $x - 10$ summed up. This means that we have $x + 3$ times $x - 10$:
$(x + 3)(x - 10) = 0$ or $(x - 10)(x + 3) = 0$

21. A
We need to simplify the equation by distributing factors and then collecting x terms on one side, and the others on the other side:
$(a + 2)x - b = -2 + (a + b)x$
$ax + 2x - b = -2 + ax + bx$

ax + 2x - ax - bx = -2 + b ... ax and -ax cancel:

2x - bx = -2 + b ... we take -1 as a factor on the right side:

(2 - b)x = -(2 - b)

x = -(2 - b)/(2 - b) ... Simplifying by 2 - b:

x = -1

22. C
To obtain a polynomial, remove the parenthesis by distributing the related factors to the terms inside the parenthesis:

$1 - x(1 - x(1 - x)) = 1 - x(1 - (x - x * x)) = 1 - x(1 - x + x^2)$

$= 1 - (x - x * x + x * x^2) = 1 - x + x^2 - x^3$ ... Writing this result in descending order of powers:

$= - x^3 + x^2 - x + 1$

23. D
To simplify the expression, remove the parenthesis by distributing the related factors to the terms inside the parenthesis:

7(2y + 8) + 1 − 4(y + 5)
= (7 * 2y + 7 * 8) + 1 - (4 * y + 4 * 5)

= 14y + 56 + 1 - 4y - 20

= 14y - 4y + 56 + 1 - 20 ... similar terms written together to ease summing/substituting.

= 10y + 37

24. D
We are given that each of the n employees earns s amount of salary weekly. This means that one employee earns s salary weekly. So; Richard has 'ns' amount of money to employ n employees for a week.

We are asked to find the number of days n employees can be employed with x amount of money. We can do simple direct proportion:

If Richard can employ 'n' employees for 7 days with 'ns' amount of money,

Richard can employ n employees for y days with x amount of money ... y is the number of days we need to find.

Cross multiply:

y = (x * 7)/(ns)

y = 7x/ns

25. A
$x^2 - 3x - 4$ ... try to separate the middle term -3x to find common factors with x^2 and -4 separately:

$x^2 + x - 4x - 4$ ... Here, x is a common factor for x^2 and x, and -4 is a common factor for -4x and -4:

= x(x + 1) - 4(x + 1) ... Here, x times x + 1 and -4 times x + 1 summed up. This means that we have x - 4 times x + 1:

= (x - 4)(x + 1) or (x + 1)(x - 4)

26. D
To solve the equation, we need the equation in the form $ax^2 + bx + c = 0$.

$(a^2 - b^2)x^2 + 2ax + 1 = 0$ is already in this form.

The quadratic formula to find the roots of a quadratic equation is:

$x_{1,2} = (-b \pm \sqrt{\Delta}) / 2a$ where $\Delta = b^2 - 4ac$ and is called the discriminant of the quadratic equation.

Basic Algebra

In our question, the equation is $(a^2 - b^2)x^2 + 2ax + 1 = 0$.

By remembering the form $ax^2 + bx + c = 0$: $a = a^2 - b^2$, $b = 2a$, $c = 1$

So, we can find the discriminant first, and then the roots of the equation:

$\Delta = b^2 - 4ac = (2a)^2 - 4(a^2 - b^2) * 1 = 4a^2 - 4a^2 + 4b^2 = 4b^2$

$x_{1,2} = (-b \pm \sqrt{\Delta}) / 2a = (-2a \pm \sqrt{4b^2}) / (2(a^2 - b^2)) = (-2a \pm 2b) / (2(a^2 - b^2))$

$= 2(-a \pm b) / (2(a^2 - b^2))$ ... We can simplify by 2:

$= (-a \pm b) / (a^2 - b^2)$

This means that the roots are,

$x_1 = (-a - b) / (a^2 - b^2)$ ... $a^2 - b^2$ is two square differences:

$x_1 = -(a + b) / ((a - b)(a + b))$ ... $(a + b)$ terms cancel:

$x_1 = -1/(a - b)$

$x_2 = (-a + b) / (a^2 - b^2)$ ... $a^2 - b^2$ is two square differences:

$x_2 = -(a - b) / ((a - b)(a + b))$ ... $(a - b)$ terms cancel:

$x_2 = -1/(a + b)$

27. A

To simplify, remove the parenthesis and see if any terms cancel:

$(a + b)(x + y) + (a - b)(x - y) - (ax + by) = ax + ay + bx + by + ax - ay - bx + by - ax - by$

Writing similar terms together:

$= ax + ax - ax + bx - bx + ay - ay + by + by - by$ ... + terms cancel - terms:

= ax + by

28. B

Let us call this number by x:

This number is increased by 2: x + 2

Then, it is multiplied by 3: 3(x + 2)

The result is 24: 3(x + 2) = 24 ... Solving this linear equation, we obtain the value of the number:

x + 2 = 24 / 3
x + 2 = 8
x = 8 − 2
x = 6

29. B

My age: x

My brother is 3 years older than me: x + 3

My father is 3 less than 2 times my age: 2x − 3

My father's age divided by 5 is equal to my brother's age divided by 3: (2x − 3) / 5 = (x + 3) / 3
By cross multiplication: 5(x + 3) = 3(2x − 3)

5x + 15 = 6x − 9
x = 24

My father's age: 2.24 − 3 = 48 − 3 = 45

30. C
There are two fractions containing x and the denominators are different. First, find a common denominator to simplify the expression. The least common multiplier of 4 and 7 is 28. Then,

$7(x - 2) / 28 - 4(3x + 5) / 28 = -3.28 / 28$ ... Since both sides are written on the denominator 28 now, we can eliminate them:

$7(x - 2) - 4(3x + 5) = -84$

$7x - 14 - 12x - 20 = -84$
$-5x = -84 + 14 + 20$
$-5x = -50$
$x = 50/5$
$x = 10$

Geometry

Basic Geometry

Cartesian Plane, Coordinate Grid and Plane

To locate points and draw lines and curves, we use the coordinate plane. It also called Cartesian coordinate plane. It is a two-dimensional surface with a coordinate grid in it, which helps us to count the units. For the counting of those units, we use x-axis (horizontal scale) and y-axis (vertical scale).

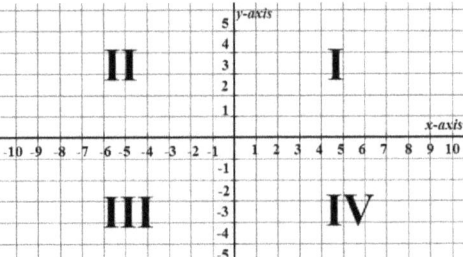

The whole system is called a coordinate system which is divided into 4 parts, called quadrants. The quadrant where all numbers are positive is the 1st quadrant (I), and if we go counterclockwise, we mark all 4 quadrants.

The location of a dot in the coordinate system is represented by coordinates. Coordinates are represented as a pair of numbers,

Geometry

where the 1st number is located on the x-axis and the 2nd number is located on the y-axis. So, if a dot A has coordinates a and b, then we write:

A = (a,b)   or   A(a,b)

The point where x-axis and y-axis intersect is called an origin. The origin is the point from which we measure the distance along the x and y axes.

In the Cartesian coordinate system we can calculate the distance between 2 given points. If we have dots with coordinates:

A = (a,b)
B = (c,d)

Then the distance d between A and B can be calculated by the following formula:

$$d = \sqrt{(c-a)^2 + (d-b)^2}$$

Cartesian coordinate system is used for the drawing of 2-dimentional shapes, and is also commonly used for functions.

Example:

Draw the function   y = (1 - x)/2

To draw a linear function, we need at least 2 points. If we put that x = 0 then value for y would be:

$$y = \frac{1-x}{2} = \frac{1-0}{2} = \frac{1}{2}$$

We found the 1st point, let's name it A, with following co-ordinates:

A = (0,1/2)

To find the 2nd point, we can put that x=1. Here, the value for y would be:

$$y = \frac{1-x}{2} = \frac{1-1}{2} = \frac{0}{2} = 0$$

If we denote the 2nd point with B, then the coordinates for this point are:

B=(1,0)

Since we have 2 points necessary for the function, we find them in the coordinate system and we connect them with a line that represents the function,

Perimeter Area and Volume

Perimeter and Area (2-dimentional shapes)

Perimeter of a shape determines the length around that shape, while the area includes the space inside the shape.

Rectangle:

$P = 2a + 2b$
$A = ab$

Square

$P = 4a$
$A = a^2$

Parallelogram

$P = 2a + 2b$
$A = ah_a = bh_b$

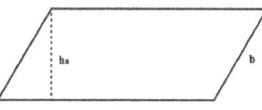

Rhombus

$P = 4a$
$A = ah = \dfrac{d_1 d_2}{2}$

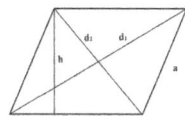

Triangle

$P = a+b+c$

$A = \dfrac{ah_a}{2} = \dfrac{bh_b}{2} = \dfrac{ch_c}{2}$

Equilateral Triangle

$P = 3a$

$A = \dfrac{a^2\sqrt{3}}{4}$

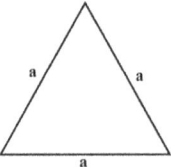

Trapezoid

$P = a+b+c+d$

$A = \dfrac{a+b}{2}h$

Circle

$P = 2r\pi$

$A = r^2\pi$

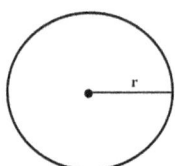

Area and Volume (3-dimentional shapes)

To calculate the area of a 3-dimentional shape, we calculate the areas of all sides and then we add them all.

To find the volume of a 3-dimentional shape, we multiply

Geometry

the area of the base (B) and the height (H) of the 3-dimentional shape.

$$V = BH$$

In case of a pyramid and a cone, the volume would be divided by 3.

$$V = BH/3$$

Here are some of the 3-dimentional shapes with formulas for their area and volume:

Cuboids

$A = 2(ab + bc + ac)$
$V = abc$

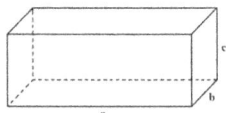

Cube

$A = 6a^2$
$V = a^3$

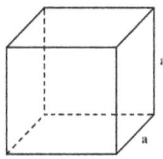

Pyramid

$A = ab + ah_a + bh_b$
$V = \dfrac{abH}{3}$

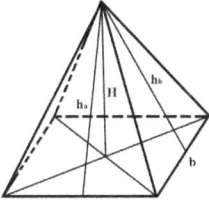

Cylinder

$$A = 2r^2\pi + 2r\pi H$$
$$V = r^2\pi H$$

Cone

$$A = (r+s)r\pi$$
$$V = \frac{r^2\pi H}{3}$$

Pythagorean Geometry

If we have a right triangle ABC, where its sides (legs) are a and b and c is a hypotenuse (the side opposite the right angle), then we can establish a relationship between these sides using the following formula:

$$c^2 = a^2 + b^2$$

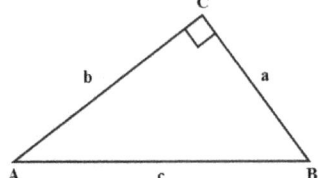

This formula is proven in the Pythagorean Theorem. There are many proofs of this theorem, but we'll look at just one geometrical proof:

If we draw squares on the right triangle's sides, then the area of the square upon the hypotenuse is equal to the sum of the areas of the squares that are upon other two sides of the triangle. Since the areas of these squares are a², b² and c², that is how we got the formula above.

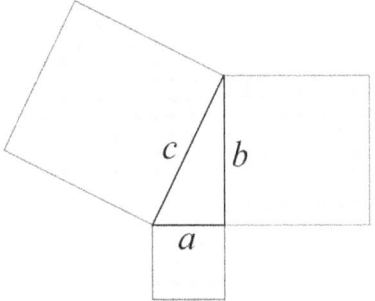

One of the famous right triangles is one with sides 3, 4 and 5. And we can see here that:

3² + 4² = 5²
9 + 16 = 25
25 = 25

Example Problem:

The isosceles triangle ABC has a perimeter of 18 centimeters, and the difference between its base and legs is 3 centimeters. Find the height of this triangle.

We write the information we have about triangle ABC and we draw a picture for a better understanding of the

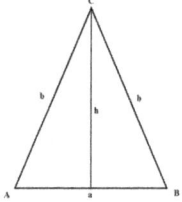

relation between its elements:
P=18 cm
a - b = 3 cm
h=?

We use the formula for the perimeter of the isosceles triangle, since that is what is given to us:
P = a + 2b = 18 cm

Notice that we have 2 equations with 2 variables, so we can solve it as a system of equations:

a + 2b = 18
a − b = 3 / a + 2b = 18
2a - 2b = 6 / a + 2b + 2a - 2b = 18 + 6
3a = 24
a = 24/3 = 8 cm

Now we go back to find b:
a - b = 3
8 - b = 3
b = 8 - 3
b = 5 cm

Using Pythagorean Theorem, we can find the height using a and b, because the height falls on the side a at the right angle. Notice that height cuts side a exactly in half, and that's why we use in the formula a/2. Here, b is our hypotenuse, so we have:

$b^2 = (a/2)^2 + h^2$
$h^2 = b^2 - (a/2)^2$
$h^2 = 5^2 - (8/2)^2$
$h^2 = 5^2 - (8/2)^2$
$h^2 = 25 - 4^2$
$h^2 = 26 - 16$
$h^2 = 9$
$h = 3$ cm.

Quadrilaterals

Quadrilaterals are 2-dimentional geometrical shapes that have 4 sides and 4 angles. There are many types of quadrilaterals, depending on the length of its sides, if they are parallel, and the size of its angles. All quadrilaterals have the following properties:

Sum of all interior angles is 360°

Sum of all exterior angles is 360°

A quadrilateral is a parallelogram is it fulfills at least one of the following conditions:

- Angles on each side are supplementary
- Opposite angles are equal
- Opposite sides are equal
- Diagonals intersect each other exactly in half

Here are some of the quadrilaterals:

Square

All sides are equal
All angles are right angles

Rectangle

2 pairs of equal sides
All angles are right angles

Parallelogram

2 pairs of equal sides
Opposite angles are equal

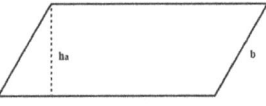

Rhombus

All sides are equal
Opposite angles are equal

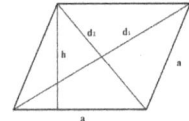

Trapezoid

One pair of parallel sides

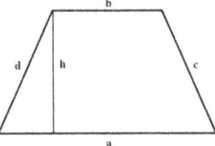

Example Problem

Find all angles of a parallelogram if one angle is greater than the other one by 40°.

First, we draw an image of a parallelogram:

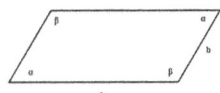

We denote angles by α and β, Since this is a parallelogram, the opposite angles are equal.

Geometry

We are given that one angle is greater than the other one by 40°, so we can write:
β = α + 40°

We solve this problem in two ways:
1) The sum of all internal angles of every quadrilateral is 360°. There are 2 α and 2 β. So we have:
2α + 2β = 360°
Now, instead of β we write α + 40:
2 α + 2 (α + 40°) =360°
2 α + 2 α + 80° = 360°
4 α = 360° - 80°
4 α = 280°
α = 280° / 4
α = 70°

Now we can find β from α:
β = α + 40°
β = 70° + 40°
β = 110°

2) One condition for parallelogram is "Angles on each side are supplementary" and we can use that to find these angles:

α + β = 180°
α + α + 40° = 180°
2 α = 180° - 40°
2 α = 140°
α = 70°

Now we find β:
β = α + 40°
β = 70° + 40°
β = 110°

Answer Sheet

	A	B	C	D	E		A	B	C	D	E
1	○	○	○	○	○	21	○	○	○	○	○
2	○	○	○	○	○	22	○	○	○	○	○
3	○	○	○	○	○	23	○	○	○	○	○
4	○	○	○	○	○	24	○	○	○	○	○
5	○	○	○	○	○	25	○	○	○	○	○
6	○	○	○	○	○	26	○	○	○	○	○
7	○	○	○	○	○	27	○	○	○	○	○
8	○	○	○	○	○	28	○	○	○	○	○
9	○	○	○	○	○	29	○	○	○	○	○
10	○	○	○	○	○	30	○	○	○	○	○
11	○	○	○	○	○						
12	○	○	○	○	○						
13	○	○	○	○	○						
14	○	○	○	○	○						
15	○	○	○	○	○						
16	○	○	○	○	○						
17	○	○	○	○	○						
18	○	○	○	○	○						
19	○	○	○	○	○						
20	○	○	○	○	○						

Geometry Practice Questions

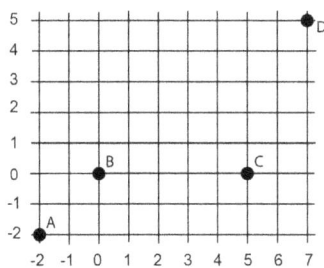

1. Which of the above points represents the origin?

    a. A
    b. B
    c. C
    d. D

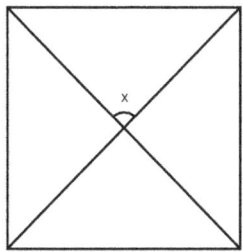

2. What is measurement of the indicated angle?

    a. 45°
    b. 90°
    c. 60°
    d. 30°

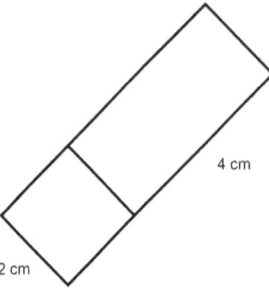

Note: figure not drawn to scale.

3. Assuming the figure with side 2 cm. is square, what is the perimeter of the above shape?

    a. 12 cm
    b. 16 cm
    c. 6 cm
    d. 20 cm

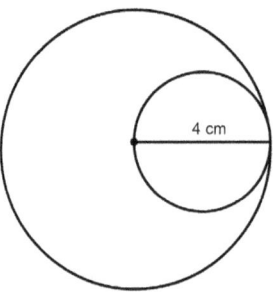

Note: Figure not drawn to scale

Geometry

4. Assuming the diameter of the small circle is the radius of the larger circle, what is (area of large circle) - (area of small circle) in the figure above?

   a. 8 π cm²
   b. 10 π cm²
   c. 12 π cm²
   d. 16 π cm²

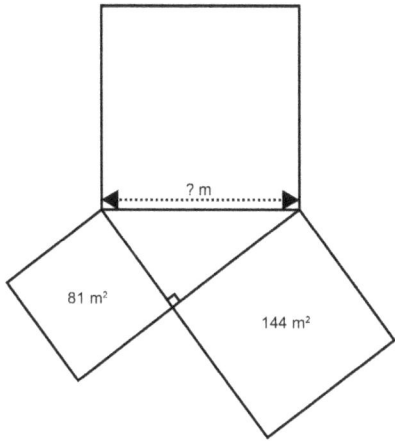

Note: Figure not drawn to scale

5. Assuming the shapes around the center right triangle are square, what is the length of each side of the indicated square above?

   a. 10
   b. 15
   c. 20
   d. 5

6. Choose the expression the figure represents.

    a. $X \leq 1$
    b. $X < 1$
    c. $X > 1$
    d. $X \geq 1$

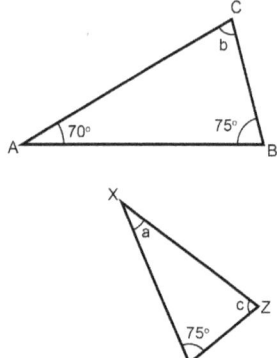

7. What are the respective values of a, b & c if both triangles are similar?

    a. 70°, 70°, 35°
    b. 70°, 35°, 70°
    c. 35°, 35°, 35°
    d. 70°, 75°, 35°

— Geometry —

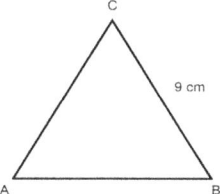

Note: figure not drawn to scale

8. What is the perimeter of the equilateral △ABC above?

    a. 18 cm
    b. 12 cm
    c. 27 cm
    d. 15 cm

Note: figure not drawn to scale

9. Assuming the 2 quadrangles are identical rectangles, what is perimeter of △ABC in the above shape?

    a. 25.5 cm
    b. 27 cm
    c. 30 cm
    d. 29 cm

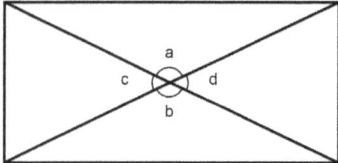

10. What is the sum of all the angles in the rectangle above?

    a. 180°
    b. 360°
    c. 90°
    d. 120°

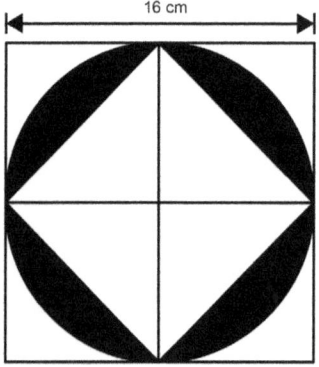

Note: figure not drawn to scale

Geometry

11. A tile factory makes custom tiles, shown above, from two types of stone. If a customer requires 200 tiles, how much black stone will be required?

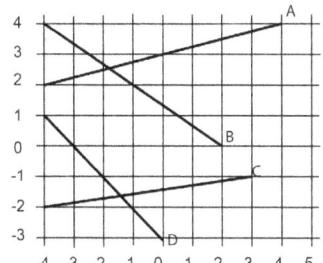

    a. 256 m²

    b. 2560 m²

    c. 2.56 m²

    d. 25.6 m²

12. Which of the lines above represents the equation 2y − x = 4?

    a. A

    b. B

    c. C

    d. D

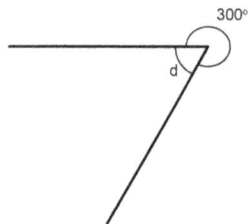

13. What is the measurement of the indicated angle?

    a. 45°
    b. 90°
    c. 60°
    d. 50°

5 cm

Note: figure not drawn to scale

14. What is the perimeter of the above shape, assuming the bottom portion is square?

    a. 22.85 cm
    b. 20 cm
    c. 15 cm
    d. 25.546 cm

Geometry

Note: Figure not drawn to scale

15. Assuming the quadrangle in the figure above is square, what is the length of the sides in the triangle above?

    a. 10
    b. 20
    c. 100
    d. 40

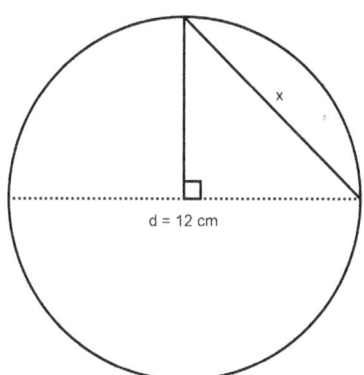

Note: Figure not drawn to scale

16. Calculate the length of side x.

   a. 6.46
   b. 8.48
   c. 3.6
   d. 6.4

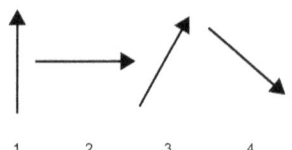

1   2   3   4

17. What is the correct order of respective slopes for the lines above?

   a. Positive, undefined, negative, positive
   b. Negative, zero, undefined, positive
   c. Undefined, zero, positive, negative
   d. Zero, positive undefined, negative

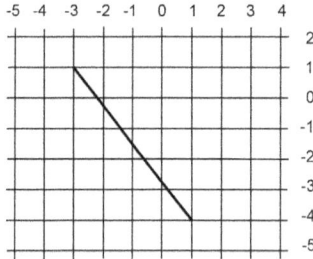

18. What is the slope of the line shown above?

   a. 5/4
   b. -4/5
   c. -5/4
   d. -4/5

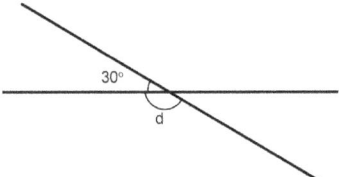

19. What is the indicated angle above?

    a. 150°
    b. 330°
    c. 60°
    d. 120°

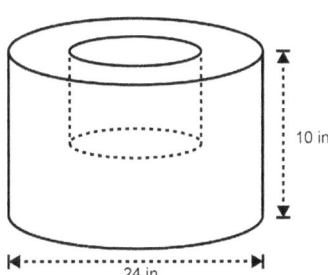

Note: figure not drawn to scale

20. What is the volume of the above solid made by a hollow cylinder that is half the size (in all dimensions) of the larger cylinder?

    a. 1440 π in³
    b. 1260 π in³
    c. 1040 π in³
    d. 960 π in³

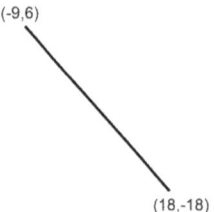

21. What is the slope of the line above?

    a. -8/9
    b. 9/8
    c. -9/8
    d. 8/9

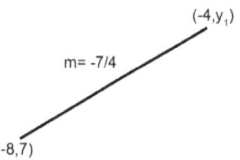

22. With the data given above, what is the value of y_1?

    a. 0
    b. -7
    c. 7
    d. 8

Geometry

Type A: 1300 ft²

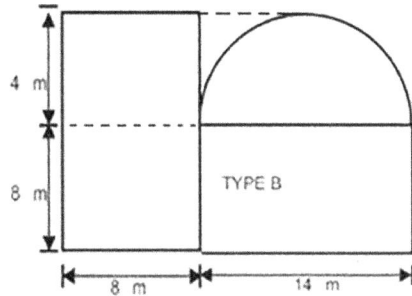

TYPE B

Note: Figure not drawn to scale

23. The price of houses in a certain subdivision is based on the total area. Susan is watching her budget and wants to choose the house with the lowest area. Which house type, A (1300 ft2) or B, should she choose if she would like the house with the lowest price? (1 m² = 10.76 ft² & π = 22/7)

 a. Type B is smaller at 140 ft²
 b. Type A is smaller
 c. Type B is smaller at 855 ft²
 d. Type B is larger

24. How much water can be stored in a cylindrical container 5 meters in diameter and 12 meters high?

Note: figure not drawn to scale

a. 235.65 m³
b. 223.65 m³
c. 240.65 m³
d. 252.65 m³

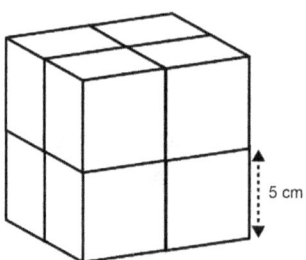

Note: figure not drawn to scale

25. Assuming the figure above is composed of cubes, what is the volume?

a. 125 cm³
b. 875 cm³
c. 1000 cm³
d. 500 cm³

26. Choose the expression the figure represents.

    a. $X > 2$
    b. $X \geq 2$
    c. $X < 2$
    d. $X \leq 2$

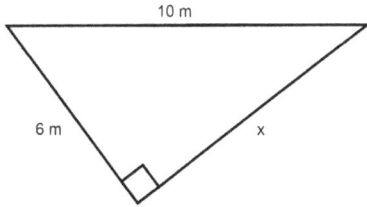

Note: figure not drawn to scale

27. What is the length of the missing side in the triangle above?

    a. 6
    b. 4
    c. 8
    d. 5

28. What is the value of the angle y?

    a. 25°
    b. 15°
    c. 30°
    d. 105°

29. What is the distance between the two points?

    a. ≈19
    b. 20
    c. ≈21
    d. ≈22

Geometry

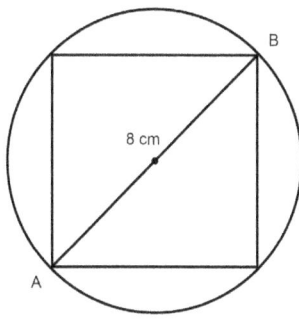

Note: figure not drawn to scale

30. What is area of the circle?

a. 4 π cm²
b. 12 π cm²
c. 10 π cm²
d. 16 π cm²

Answer Key

1. A

Point A represents the origin.

2. A

The diagonals of a square intersect at right angles, so each angle measures 90°. Half of that angle will be 45°

3. B

We see that there is a square with side 2 cm and a rectangle adjacent to it, with one side 2 cm (common side with the square) and the other side 4 cm. The perimeter of a shape is found by summing up all sides surrounding the shape, not adding the ones inside the shape. Three 2 cm sides from the square, and two 4 cm sides and one 2 cm side from the rectangle contribute the perimeter.

So, the perimeter of the shape is: 2 + 2 + 2 + 4 + 2 + 4 = 16 cm.

4. C

We are given a large circle and a small circle inside it; with the diameter equal to the radius of the large one. The diameter of the small circle is 4 cm. This means that its radius is 2 cm. Since the diameter of the small circle is the radius of the large circle, the radius of the large circle is 4 cm. The area of a circle is calculated by: πr^2 where r is the radius.

Area of the small circle: $\pi(2)^2 = 4\pi$

Area of the large circle: $\pi(4)^2 = 16\pi$

The difference area is found by:

Area of the large circle - Area of the small circle = $16\pi - 4\pi = 12\pi$

Geometry

5. B

We see that there are three squares forming a right triangle in the middle. Two of the squares have the areas 81 m² and 144 m². If we denote their sides a and b respectively:

$a^2 = 81$ and $b^2 = 144$. The length, which is asked, is the hypotenuse; a and b are the opposite and adjacent sides of the right angle. By using the Pythagorean Theorem, we can find the value of the asked side:

Pythagorean Theorem:

$(Hypotenuse)^2 = (Opposite\ Side)^2 + (Adjacent\ Side)^2$

$h^2 = a^2 + b^2$

$a^2 = 81$ and $b^2 = 144$ are given. So;

$h^2 = 81 + 144$

$h^2 = 225$

$h = 15$ m

6. B

The line is pointing towards numbers less than 1. The equation is therefore, $X < 1$.

7. D

Comparing respective angles - 70°, 75°, 35°

8. C

Equilateral triangle with 9 cm. sides
Perimeter = 9 + 9 + 9 = 27 cm.

9. D

Perimeter of triangle ABC is asked.
Perimeter of a triangle = sum of all three sides.

Here, Perimeter of △ABC = |AC| + |CB| + |AB|.

Since the triangle is located in the middle of two adjacent and identical rectangles, we find the side lengths using these rectangles:

|AB| = 6 + 6 = 12 cm

|CB| = 8.5 cm

|AC| = |CB| = 8.5 cm

Perimeter = |AC| + |CB| + |AB| = 8.5 + 8.5 + 12 = 29 cm

10. B
a + b + c + d = ?
The sum of angles around a point is 360°
a + b + c + d = 360°

11. A
Black stone for 200 tiles = 200 x [Total tile area – Inner white area(4 triangles)]

= 200 x [(16^2) - (4 x 1/2 x 8 x 8)]

= 200 x (256 - 128) = 200 x 128 = 25600 cm^2

Converting to meters – 1 cm. = 0.01 meters

= 25600/100 m^2

= 256 m^2

12. A
If a line represents an equation, all points on that line should satisfy the equation. Meaning that all (x, y) pairs present on the line should be able to verify that 2y - x is equal to 4. We can find out the correct line by trying a (x, y) point existing on each line. It is easier to choose points on the intersection of the grid lines:

Let us try the point (4, 4) on line A:

2 * 4 - 4 = 4

8 - 4 = 4

4 = 4 ... this is a correct result, so the equation for line A is 2y - x = 4.

Let us try other points to check the other lines:

Point (-1, 2) on line B:

2 * 2 - (-1) = 4

4 + 1 = 4

5 = 4 ... this is a wrong result, so the equation for line B is not 2y - x = 4.

Point (3, -1) on line C:

2 * (-1) - 3 = 4

-2 - 3 = 4

-5 = 4 ... this is a wrong result, so the equation for line C is not 2y - x = 4.

Point (-2, -1) on line D:

2 * (-1) - (-2) = 4

-2 + 2 = 4

0 = 4 ... this is a wrong result, so the equation for line D is not 2y - x = 4.

13. C
The sum of angles around a point is 360°

d + 300 = 360°

d = 60°

14. A
Find the perimeter of a shape made by merging a square

and a semi circle. Perimeter = 3 sides of the square + 1/2 circumference of the circle.

= (3 x 5) + 1/2 (5 π)

= 15 + 2.5 π

= 15 + 7.853975

Perimeter = 22.85 cm

15. A

If we call one side of the square "a," the area of the square will be a^2.

We know that $a^2 = 200$ cm².

On the other hand; there is an isosceles right triangle. Using the **Pythagorean Theorem:**

(Hypotenuse)² = (Adjacent Side)² + (Opposite Side)²
Where the hypotenuse is equal to one side of the square. So,

$a^2 = x^2 + x^2$

$200 = 2x^2$

$200/2 = 2x^2/2$

$100 = x^2$

$x = \sqrt{100}$

x = 10 cm

16. B

In the question, we have a right triangle formed inside the circle. We are asked to find the length of the hypotenuse of this triangle. We can find the other two sides of the triangle by using circle properties:

The diameter of the circle is equal to 12 cm. The legs of

the right triangle are the radii of the circle; so they are 6 cm long.

Using the Pythagorean Theorem:

(Hypotenuse)² = (Adjacent Side)² + (Opposite Side)²

$x^2 = r^2 + r^2$

$x^2 = 6^2 + 6^2$

$x^2 = 72$

$x = \sqrt{72}$

$x = 8.48$

17. C
Undefined, zero, positive, negative.

18. C
Slope (m) = change in y / change in x

$(x_1, y_1) = (-3, 1)$ & $(x_2, y_2) = (1, -4)$

Slope = [-4 - 1]/[1-(-3)] = -5/4

19. A
The angles opposite both angles 30° and angle d are respectively equal to vertical angles.

2(30° + d) = 360°

2d = 360° - 60°

2d = 300°

d = 150°

20. B
Total Volume = Volume of large cylinder - Volume of small cylinder

Volume of a cylinder = area of base * height = $\pi r^2 * h$

Total Volume = $(\pi * 12^2 * 10) - (\pi * 6^2 * 5) = 1440\pi - 180\pi$

= 1260π in^3

21. A

If we know the coordinates of two points on a line, we can find the slope (m) with the below formula:

$m = (y_2 - y_1)/(x_2 - x_1)$ where (x_1, y_1) represent the coordinates of one point and (x_2, y_2) the other.

In this question:

$(-9, 6) : x_1 = -9, y_1 = 6$

$(18, -18) : x_2 = 18, y_2 = -18$

Inserting these values into the formula:

$m = (-18 - 6)/(18 - (-9)) = (-24)/(27)$ ... Simplifying by 3:

$m = -8/9$

22. A

If we know the coordinates of two points on a line, we can find the slope (m) with the below formula:

$m = (y_2 - y_1)/(x_2 - x_1)$ where (x_1, y_1) represent the coordinates of one point and (x_2, y_2) the other.

In this question:

$(-4, y_1) : x_1 = -4, y_1$ = we will find

$(-8, 7) : x_2 = -8, y_2 = 7$

$m = -7/4$

Inserting these values into the formula:

$-7/4 = (7 - y_1)/(-8 - (-4))$

$-7/4 = (7 - y_1)/(-8 + 4)$

$7/(-4) = (7 - y_1)/(-4)$ ... Simplifying the denominators of both sides by -4:

$7 = 7 - y_1$

$0 = -y_1$

$y_1 = 0$

23. D
Area of Type B consists of two rectangles and a half circle. We can find these three areas and sum them up to find the total area:

Area of the left rectangle: $(4 + 8) * 8 = 96$ m²

Area of the right rectangle: $14 * 8 = 112$ m²

The diameter of the circle is equal to 14 m. So, the radius is 14/2 = 7:

Area of the half circle = $(1/2) * \pi r^2 = (1/2) * (22/7) * (7)^2 = (1 * 22 * 49) / (2 * 7) = 77$ m²

Area of Type B = 96 + 112 + 77 = 285 m²

Converting this area to ft²: 285 m² = 285 * 10.76 ft² = 3066.6 ft²

Type B is (3066.6 - 1300 = 1766.6 ft²) 1766.6 ft² larger than type A.

24. A
The formula of the volume of cylinder is the base area multiplied by the height. As the formula:

Volume of a cylinder = $\pi r^2 h$. Where π is 3.142, r is radius of the cross sectional area, and h is the height.

We know that the diameter is 5 meters, so the radius is 5/2 = 2.5 meters.

The volume is: V = 3.142 * 2.5² * 12 = 235.65 m³.

25. C

The large cube is made up of 8 smaller cubes with 5 cm sides. The volume of a cube is found by the third power of the length of one side.

Volume of the large cube = Volume of the small cube * 8

$= (5^3) * 8 = 125 * 8$

$= 1000$ cm³

There is another solution for this question. Find the side length of the large cube. There are two cubes rows with 5 cm length for each. So, one side of the large cube is 10 cm.

The volume of this large cube is equal to $10^3 = 1000$ cm³

26. A

The line is pointing towards numbers greater than 2. The equation is therefore, $X > 2$.

27. C

Pythagorean Theorem:

$(Hypotenuse)^2 = (Perpendicular)^2 + (Base)^2$

$h^2 = a^2 + b^2$

Given: $a = 6$, $h = 10$

$h^2 = a^2 + b^2$

$b^2 = h^2 - a^2$

$b^2 = 10^2 + 6^2$

$b^2 = 100 - 36$

$b^2 = 64$

$b = 8$

28. D
Two parallel lines intersected by a third line with angles of 75°

$x = 75°$ (corresponding angles)

$x + y = 180°$ (supplementary angles)

$y = 180° - 75°$

$y = 105°$

29. D
The distance between two points is found by

$= [(x_2 - x_1)^2 + (y_2 - y_1)^2]^{1/2}$

In this question:

$(18, 12) : x_1 = 18, y_1 = 12$

$(9, -6) : x_2 = 9, y_2 = -6$

Distance $= [(9 - 18)^2 + (-6 - 12)^2]^{1/2}$

$= [(-9)^2 + (-18)^2]^{1/2}$

$= (9^2 + 2^2 * 9^2)^{1/2}$

$= (9^2(1 + 5))^{1/2}$ ... We can take 9 out of the square root:

$= 9 * 5^{1/2}$

$= 9\sqrt{5}$

$= 9 * 2.45$

$= 22.05$

The distance is approximately 22 units.

30. D
We have a circle given with diameter 8 cm and a square located within the circle. We are asked to find the area of the circle for which we only need to know the length of the radius that is the half of the diameter.

Area of circle = πr^2 ... r = 8/2 = 4 cm

Area of circle = π * 4^2

= 16π cm^2 ... As we notice, the inner square has no role in this question.

Speed, Force and Momentum

In physics, acceleration is the rate at which the velocity of a body changes with time. For example, an object such as a car that starts from a full stop, then travels in a straight line at increasing speed, is accelerating in the direction of travel. If the car changes direction at constant speed, there is strictly speaking an acceleration, although not described as such; passengers in the car will experience a force pushing them back into their seats in linear acceleration, and a sideways force on changing direction. If the speed of the car decreases, or decelerates, mathematically it is acceleration in the opposite direction.

The formula for acceleration = $A = (V_F - V_0)/t$ and is measured in meters per second^2. Here is a typical question:

A car starts from standing top and in 10 seconds is traveling 20/meters per second. What is the acceleration?

0.5 m/sec^2
1.5 m/sec^2
1 m/sec^2
2 m/sec^2

The formula for acceleration = A = $(V_f - V_0)/t$
so A = (20 m/sec - 0 m/sec)/10 sec = 2 m/sec²

Speed

Speed is the rate of change of an objects position, or, speed = (total distance traveled)/(total time taken).

Here is a typical question:

A rocket travels 3000 meters in 5 seconds. How fast is it traveling?

a. 100 m/sec
b. 200 m/sec
c. 500 m/sec
d. 600 m/sec

Answer: D
speed = (total distance traveled)/(total time taken)
3000/5 = 600 meters per second.

Force

An everyday definition of Force is the push or pull. The more scientific definition of Force is any influence that causes an object to change its movement or direction. Force is measured in Newtons, (usually N) named after Sir Isaac Newton, and his formulation of the Second Law of motion, F = ma, where F = force, m = mass and a = acceleration.

1 N = 1 kg m/s².

Therefore,

Force = Mass times Acceleration Measured in Newtons.

Acceleration is the change in speed over time.

Speed is the change in position over time.

Here is a typical question:

How much force is needed to accelerate a car that weights 500 kg to 10 m/s^2?

Force = Mass times Acceleration Measured in Newtons.

F = 500 X 10 = 50,000 N

Momentum

Momentum can be described as the sum product of the mass of an object and its velocity. This means that momentum measures the force produced by an object's mass and velocity.

The formula for calculating momentum is =
Momentum = mass X velocity

Or

P = MV

Where P = momentum, V = velocity and M = mass

Clearly the momentum of a car and a bicycle both traveling at 20 m/s will not be the same, since, although the velocity of the two objects are the same, their mass is different. The car would have greater momentum, due to its larger mass.

Note that:

The SI unit for velocity = m/s
SI unit for Mass = kg
Therefore momentum = kg x m/s and SI unit for momentum is kg x m/s
Momentum must always have a direction and so the final answer must reflect the direction of the momentum or velocity.

Sample questions

1. Find the momentum of a round stone weighing 12.05 kg rolling down a hill at 8m/s.

Formula: P = kg x m/s
= 12.05kg x 8m/s
= 96.4 kg x m/s downhill

Note the final answer has the proper SI unit of momentum (kg x m/s) after it, and it also mentions the direction of the movement.

2. A cannon ball weighing 35kg is shot from a cannon towards the east at 220 m/s, calculate the momentum of the cannon ball.

Formula - P= kg x m/s
= 35kg x 220m/s
= 7700 kg x m/s east

Answer Sheet

	A	B	C	D
1	○	○	○	○
2	○	○	○	○
3	○	○	○	○
4	○	○	○	○
5	○	○	○	○
6	○	○	○	○
7	○	○	○	○
8	○	○	○	○
9	○	○	○	○
10	○	○	○	○

1. Three cars are traveling down an even road at a velocity of 110 m/s, calculate the car with the highest momentum if they are all moving at the same speed, but the first car weighs 2500kg, second car weighs 2650kg and third car weighs 2009kg?

   a. First car
   b. Second car
   c. Third car
   d. All have same momentum

2. What is the momentum of a log of wood that weighs 700kg rolling down a hill at 4.6m/s.

   a. 3220 kg x m/s downhill
   b. 3320 kg x m/s
   c. 3320 downhill
   d. 3320 M

3. An object that weighs 500g is rolling along the road at 3.5m/s, what is the momentum of the object?

   a. 124.9 kg x m/s along road
   b. 17. 50 kg x m/s along road
   c. 1750 kg x m/s along road
   d. 1.75 kg x m/s along road

4. A javelin is thrown into a field at 18m/s. If the Javelin weighs 1.5kg, what is the momentum?

   a. 1.2 kg x m/s into the field
   b. 12 kg x m/s into the field
   c. 27 kg x m/s into the field
   d. 2.7 kg x m/s into the field

― Speed and Momentum ―

5. Which of these object has greater momentum, a 2kg truck moving east at 3.5m/s, or a 4.3kg truck moving south at 1.5m/s?

    a. First truck at 7 kg x m/s moving east
    b. Second truck at 7.45 kg x m/s due south
    c. First truck at 6.45 kg x m/s due east
    d. Second truck at 7 kg x m/s due south

6. A bullet weighing 350g is shot towards a target at a velocity of 250m/s. Calculate the momentum.

    a. 1.4 kg x m/s towards target
    b. 87.5 kg x m/s towards target
    c. 87500 kg x m/s towards target
    d. 8.75 kg x m/s towards target

7. A car starts from a full top and in 20 seconds is traveling 10/m per second. What is the acceleration?

    a. 0.5 m/sec^2
    b. 0.24 m/sec^2
    c. 1 m/sec^2
    d. 1.5 m/sec^2

8. A motorcycle traveling 90mph accelerates to pass a truck. Five seconds later, the motorcycle is going 120mph. Calculate the motorcycles' acceleration

    a. 6 mph/second
    b. 10 mph/second
    c. 15 mph/second
    d. 20 mph/second

9. The space station travels 1000 meters in 5 seconds. How fast is it traveling?

    a. 200 m/sec

    b. 400 m/sec

    c. 500 m/sec

    d. 550 m/sec

10. A runner can sprint 6 meters per second. How far will she travel in 2 minutes?

    a. 120 meters

    b. 720 meters

    c. 1200 meters

    d. 500 meters

– Speed and Momentum –

Answer Key

1. C
Momentum is a product of velocity and mass. If they are all traveling at the same speed, the car that weighs the most would have the highest momentum.

2. A
700 X 4.6 = 3220 kg x m/s downhill

3. D
First convert 500g to kg = 500/1000 = 0.5kg, momentum = 0.5 x 3.5 = 1.75 kg x m/s along the road.

4. C
p = 1.5 x 18 = 27 kg x m/s into the field

5. A
Momentum of first object = 2 x 3.5 = 7; momentum of second truck = 4.3 x 1.5 = 6.45. First truck has more momentum at 7 kg x m/s moving east.

6. B
First convert 350g to kg = 350/1000 = 0.35kg. Momentum of bullet = 0.35 x 250 = 87.5 kg x m/s towards target

7. A
The formula for acceleration = $A = (V_F - V_0)/t$

so A = (10 m/sec - 0 m/sec)/20 sec = 0.5 m/sec²

8. A
The formula for acceleration = $A = (V_F - V_0)/t$

so A = (120 - 90)/5 sec = 6 mph/second

9. A
Speed = (total distance traveled)/(total time taken)
1000/5 = 200 meters per second

10. B
Speed = (total distance traveled)/(total time taken)

6 = x/120   (convert minutes to seconds)

6 * 120 = x

X = 720 meters

Mode, Mean and Median

The Mode, Mean and Median, are types of averages.

The mean is the average calculated by adding the numbers and dividing by the number of items in the data set. The median is the middle value in a data set. To calculate the median, put the numbers in order, and the median will be the middle number. If there is an even number of items in the data set, then the median is found by taking the mean (average) of the two middlemost numbers. See our example below. The mode is the most frequently occurring number. If no number is repeated, then there is no mode.

Examples

Find the median, mode and mean of the following list:
6, 7, 8, 12, 14, 6, 7, 10

Find the mean

First add the numbers
6 + 7 + 8 + 12 + 14 + 6 + 7 + 10 = 70
There are 8 numbers in the list, so divide by 9
70/8 = 8.75 = mean

Find the median

First put the numbers in order
6, 6, 7, 7, 8, 10, 12, 14,

The data set has an even number of numbers, so the median is the average of 7 and 8. (7 + 8)/2 = 7.5

Find the mode

The mode is the most frequently occurring number. Here 6 and 7 both occur twice, so they are both considered the mode.

Answer Sheet

	A	B	C	D
1	○	○	○	○
2	○	○	○	○
3	○	○	○	○
4	○	○	○	○
5	○	○	○	○
6	○	○	○	○
7	○	○	○	○
8	○	○	○	○
9	○	○	○	○
10	○	○	○	○

Practice Questions

1. Find the median of the set of numbers: 1,2,3,4,5,6,7,8,9 and 10.

    a. 55
    b. 10
    c. 1
    d. 5.5

2. Find the median of the set of numbers: 21, 3, 7, 17, 19, 31, 46, 20 and 43.

    a. 19
    b. 20
    c. 3
    d. 167

3. Find the median of the set of numbers: 100, 200, 450, 29, 1029, 300 and 2001.

    a. 300
    b. 29
    c. 7
    d. 4,080

4. The following represents the age distribution of students in an elementary class. Find the mode of the values: 7, 9, 10, 13, 11, 7, 9, 19, 12, 11, 9, 7, 9, 10, 11.

    a. 7
    b. 9
    c. 10
    d. 11

5. Find the mode from these test results: 90, 80, 77, 86, 90, 91, 77, 66, 69, 65, 43, 65, 75, 43, 90.

    a. 43
    b. 77
    c. 65
    d. 90

6. Find the mode from these test results: 17, 19, 18, 17, 18, 19, 11, 17, 16, 19, 15, 15, 15, 17, 13, 11.

    a. 15
    b. 11
    c. 17
    d. 19

7. Find the mean of these set of numbers: 100, 1050, 320, 600 and 150.

    a. 333
    b. 444
    c. 440
    d. 320

8. The following numbers represent the ages of people on a bus: 3, 6, 27, 13, 6, 8, 12, 20, 5, 10. Calculate their mean of their ages.

    a. 11
    b. 6
    c. 9
    d. 110

9. The following are the number of people who attend church every Friday for 7 weeks: 62, 18, 39, 13, 16, 37, 25. Find the mean.

    a. 25
    b. 210
    c. 62
    d. 30

10. What number would you divide by to calculate the mean of 6, 8, 9, and 11?

    a. 2
    b. 3
    c. 4
    d. 5

Answer Key

1. D
First arrange the numbers in a numerical sequence – 1,2,3,4,5,6,7,8,9, 10. Then find the middle number or numbers. The middle numbers are 5 and 6. The median = 5 + 6/2 = 11/2 = 5.5

2. B
First arrange the numbers in a numerical sequence – 3,7, 17, 19, 20, 21, 31, 43, 46. Next find the middle number. The median = 20

3. A
First arrange the numbers in a numerical sequence – 29,100, 200, 300, 450, 1029, 2001. Next find the middle number. The median = 300

4. B
Simply find the most recurring number. The most occurring number in the series is 9

5. D
Simply find the most recurring number. The most occurring number in the series is 90.

6. C
Simply find the most recurring number. The most occurring number in the series is 15.

7. B
First add all the numbers 100 + 1050 + 320 + 600 + 150 = 2220. Then divide by 5 (the number of data provided) = 2220/5 = 444

8. A
First add all the numbers 3 + 6 + 27 + 13 + 6 + 8 + 12 + 20 + 5 + 10 = 110. Then divide by 10 (the number of data provided) = 110/10 = 11

9. D
First add all the numbers 62 + 18 + 39 + 13 + 16 + 37 + 25 = 210. Then divide by 7 (the number of data provided) = 210/7 = 30

10. C
To calculate the mean of 6, 8, 9, and 11, divide by 4.

How to Answer Basic Math Questions - the Basics

First, read the problem, but not the answers.

Work through the problem first and come up with your own answers. Hopefully, you should find your answer among the choices.

If no answer matches the one you got, re-check your math, but this time, use a different method. In math, there are different ways to solve a problem.

Math Multiple Choice Strategy

The two strategies for working with basic math multiple choice are Estimation and Elimination.

Estimation is just as it sounds - try to estimate an approximate answer first. Then look at the choices.

Elimination is probably the most powerful strategy for answering multiple choice.

Eliminate obviously incorrect answers and narrowing the possible choices.

Here are a few basic math examples of how this works.

Solve 2/3 + 5/12

a. 9/17

b. 3/11

c. 7/12

d. 1 1/12

First estimate the answer. 2/3 is more than half and 5/12 is about half, so the answer is going to be very close to 1.

Next, Eliminate. Choice A is about 1/2 and can be eliminated, choice B is very small, less than 1/2 and can be eliminated. Choice C is close to 1/2 and can be eliminated. Leaving only choice D, which is just over 1.

Work through the solution, find a common denominator and add. The correct answer is 1 1/12, so Choice D is correct.

Let's look at another example:

Solve 4/5 – 2/3

a. 2/2
b. 2/13
c. 1
d. 2/15

First, quickly estimate the answer. 4/5 is very close to 1, and 2/3 more than half, so the answer is going to be less than 1/2.

Choice A can be eliminated right away, because it is 1.

Choice C can be eliminated for the same reason.

Next, look at the denominators. Since 5 and 3 don't go into 13, choice B can be eliminated as well. That leaves choice D. Checking the answer, the common denominator will be 15. So the answer is 2/15 and choice D is correct.

Fractions Shortcut - Canceling Out

In any operation with fractions, if the numerator of one fraction has a common multiple with the denominator of the other, you can cancel out. This saves time and simplifies the problem quickly, making it easier to manage.

Solve 2/15 ÷ 4/5

    a. 6/65

    b. 6/75

    c. 5/12

    d. 1/6

To divide fractions, we multiply the first fraction with the inverse of the second fraction. Therefore we have 2/15 x 5/4. The numerator of the first fraction, 2, shares a multiple with the denominator of the second fraction, 4, which is 2. These cancel out, which gives, 1/3 x 1/2 = 1/6

Canceling Out solved the questions very quickly, but we can still use multiple choice strategies to answer.

Choice B can be eliminated because 75 is too large a denominator. Choice C can be eliminated because 5 and 15 don't go into 12.

Choice D is correct.

Decimal Multiple Choice Strategy and Short-cuts

Multiplying decimals gives a very quick way to estimate and eliminate choices. Anytime that you multiply decimals, it is going to give an answer with the same number of decimal places as the combined operands.

So for example,

2.38 X 1.2 will produce a number with three places of decimal, which is 2.856.
Here are a few examples with step-by-step explanation:

Solve 2.06 x 1.2

    a. 24.82

    b. 2.482

    c. 24.72

    d. 2.472

This is a simple question, but even before you start calculating, you can eliminate several choices. When multiplying decimals, there will always be as many numbers behind the decimal place in the answer as the sum of the ones in the initial problem, so choices A and C can be eliminated.

The correct answer is D: 2.06 x 1.2 = 2.472

Basic Math Multiple Choice

Solve 20.0 ÷ 2.5

    a. 12.05

    b. 9.25

    c. 8.3

    d. 8

First estimate the answer to be around 10, and eliminate choice A. And since it'd also be an even number, you can eliminate choices B and C, leaving only choice D.

The correct Answer is D: 20.0 ÷ 2.5 = 8

How to Study for a Math Test

EVERY SUBJECT HAS ITS OWN PARTICULAR STUDY METHOD. Math is mostly numerical, rather than verbal, and requires logical thinking; it has its own way to be studied. Before touching on significant points of studying a math test, lets look at some of the fundamentals of "learning."

Learning is not an instant experience; it is a procedure. Learning is a process not an event. Rome wasn't built in a day, and learning anything (or everything) isn't going to happen in a day either. You cannot expect to learn everything in one day, at night, before the test. It is important and necessary to learn day-by-day. Good time management plays a considerable role in learning. When you manage your time, and begin test preparation well in advance, you will notice the subjects are easier than you thought, or feared, and you will take the test without the stress of a sleepless body and an anxious mind.

Memorizing is a temporary step of learning if information is not comprehended and applied afterwards. Memorize just the basics and understand the meaning; then apply, analyze, synthesize and evaluate.

These are the hierarchical layout of cognitive learning: Of course, there are some basic properties that you need to memorize in the beginning, since you cannot prove the facts every time you solve a math test. For example; the inner angles of a triangle sum up to 180°. If you do not know this, you may not be able to solve triangle problems. And, more important, if you do not practice, you will certainly forget it. Practice helps information take root in your brain. Applying the same property to various types of questions extends the roots.

For example, if you see a triangle, you can analyze the question by the property. In a question, if you see a hexagon, you can split it into triangles and use the property, called synthesizing followed by evaluation. Following these steps, the property is completely learned and has its place in your long term memory.

A useful method in providing consistent learning is using similarities between the information and events, images, shapes, … etc. For example, assume that you have difficulty remembering the formula
$x^a/y^b = x^a y^{-b} = 1/(x^{-a} y^b)$.

You can associate this to an elevator: The exponents changing location (numerator/denominator) need to change exponent sign, similarly, people going up need to push the up button and if they decide to go down, they need to push the down button; so they need to change the button. Also; writing the formula in large letters and sticking it on a surface that is frequently visible helps memorizing it by using visual intelligence. The more senses (visual, musical, auditory, logical, …) the material is associated with, the more permanent it is.

Attend to all classes. Knowledge is not replaceable by others, and every brain is unique. You cannot learn math from your classmate's notes; take your own notes in your own understanding of the material. What you understand, or don't understand, and how you understand it is different to everyone else. Highlight the important points in your own way. Remember math and all other courses are mostly learned at school - practice comes afterwards at home.

Find your own way of learning. Every person learns and studies differently. Some take notes, some do not like writing; listening is the major way of embracing information for them, and some watch. It is important to detect the way that is more useful for you. Coloring important points also helps. Due to selective perception; we see the attractive words, signs before the rest. While studying math, make a list; first, determine the subjects you feel inadequate on and focus on them initially.

Never gloss over something that you do not fully understand. Information is built on previous learning in a hierarchical order. If you have questions about a mathematical property, and don't understand it completely, you cannot solve problems using that property. This true for any subject, but especially for math. You need to have a strong background to succeed in math. You need to know your basic math inside out to do algebra. And you need to know your algebra inside out to do calculus. If you do not know exponentials, you cannot solve logarithms. If you don't understand something, get help from your teachers, reread course materials, follow the examples in the textbook from start to finish, discuss with friends or hire a private tutor. Never skip over something that you don't understand – it will come back to haunt you!

Practice makes perfect! Yes – it really does! Working through math problems in your own way is essential. Looking over examples is a good first step – but only that. The example solutions shown in the textbook show you have to solve a problem, next you have to do it yourself. Completing assignments and practice questions are critical. You see different types of examples and acquire different outlooks when facing math problems. Math is fun because usually there are many ways to reach the solution. Find alternative ways to solve a problem to anchors your learning deeper. Find similar and different problems, discuss with friends, ask each other questions. Observing other people's way of thinking, and solving problems will help both of you improves.

Succeeding in math is a mental action. However, do not disregard physical and psychological effects. Always think positive and never give up; no success is gained without effort. Of course, you will waste time solving problems you find easy, and you will struggle with difficult problems. In the end, you will be one step further ahead. And then after more time spent practicing, you will be another step ahead.

Reward yourself after intense studies. This will keep your motivation high. The reward may be a chocolate bar, playing a game for 20 minutes, or taking a walk in the park. It is very essential to have a good night's sleep before taking a math test. Eating habits directly effect success. Keep away from fast food as much as you can, eat a light meal before a test. Finally, keep your inner motivation very high. Believe in yourself; you will certainly get the good result from planned, efficient studies.

How to Prepare for a Test

Most students hide their heads and procrastinate when faced with preparing for an exam, hoping that somehow they will be spared the agony, especially if it is a big one that their futures rely on. Avoiding a test is what many students do best and unfortunately, they suffer the consequences because of their lack of preparation.

Test preparation requires strategy and dedication. It is the perfect training ground for a professional life. Besides having several reliable strategies, successful students also has a clear goal and know how to accomplish it. These tried and true concepts have worked well and will make your test preparation easier.

Test Prep and Study Skills Video Tutorials

https://www.test-preparation.ca/test-video/

The Study Approach

Take responsibility for your own test preparation.

It is a common - but big - mistake to link your studying to someone else's. Study partners are great, but only if they are reliable. It is your job to be prepared for the test, even if a study partner fails you. Do not allow others to distract you from your goals.

Prioritize the time available to study

When do you learn best, early in the day or at night? Does your mind absorb and retain information most efficiently in small blocks of time, or do you require long stretches to get the most done? It is important to figure out the best blocks of time available to you when you can be the most productive. Try to consolidate activities to allow for longer periods of study time.

Find a quiet place where you will not be disturbed

Do not try to squeeze in quality study time in any old location. Find a peaceful place with a minimum of distractions, such as the library, a park or even the laundry room. Good lighting is essential and you need to have comfortable seating and a desk surface large enough to hold your materials. It is probably not a great idea to study in your bedroom. You might be distracted by clothes on the floor, a book you have been planning to read, the telephone or something else. Besides, in the middle of studying, that bed will start to look very comfortable. Whatever you do, avoid using the bed as a place to study since you might fall asleep to avoiding studying!

The exception is flashcards. By far the most productive study time is sitting down and studying and studying only. However, with flashcards you can carry them with you and make use of odd moments, like standing in line or waiting for the bus. This isn't as productive, but it really helps and is definitely worth doing.

Determine what you need to study

Gather together your books, your notes, your laptop and any other materials needed to focus on your study for this exam. Ensure you have everything you need so you don't waste time. Remember paper, pencils and erasers, sticky notes, bottled water and a snack. Keep your phone with you if you need it to find essential information, but keep it turned off so others can't distract you.

Have a positive attitude

It is essential that you approach your studies for the test with an attitude that says you will pass it. And pass it with flying colors! This is one of the most important keys to successful studying. Believing that you are capable helps you to become capable.

The Strategy of Studying

Review class notes

Stay on top of class notes and assignments by reviewing them frequently and regularly. Re-writing notes can be a terrific study trick, as it helps lock in information. Pay special attention to any comments that have been made by the teacher. If a study guide has been made available as part of the class materials, use it! It will be a valuable tool to use for studying.

Estimate how much time you will need

If you are concerned about the amount of time you have available it is a good idea to set up a schedule so that you do not get bogged down on one section and end without enough time left to study other things. Remember to schedule break time, and use that time for a little exercise or other stress reducing techniques.

Test yourself to determine your weaknesses

Look online for additional assessment and evaluation tools available for a particular subject. Visit our website https://www.test-preparation.ca for test tips and more practice questions. Once you have determined areas of concern, you will be able to focus on studying the information they contain and just brush up on the other areas of the exam.

Mental Prep – How to Psych Yourself Up for a Test

Since tests are often a big factor in your final grade or acceptance into a program, it is understandable that taking tests creates anxiety for many students. Even students who know they have learned the required material find their minds going blank as they stare at the test booklet. One easy way to overcome that anxiety is to prepare mentally for the test. Here are a few simple techniques.

Do not procrastinate

Study the material for the test when it becomes available, and continue to review the material until the test day. By waiting until the last minute and trying to cram for the test the night before, you actually increase anxiety. This leads to an increase in negative self-talk. Telling yourself "I can't learn this. I am going to fail" is a pretty sure indication that you are right. At best, your performance on the test will not be as strong if you have procrastinated instead of studying.

Positive self-talk.

Positive self-talk drowns out negative self-talk and to increases your confidence level. Whenever you begin feeling overwhelmed or anxious about the test, remind yourself that you have studied enough, you know the material and that you will pass the test. Both negative and positive self-talk are really just your fantasy, so why not choose to be a winner?

Do not compare yourself to others.

Do not compare yourself to other students. Instead, focus on your strengths and weaknesses and prepare accordingly. Regardless of how others perform, your performance is the only one that matters to your grade. Comparing yourself to others increases your anxiety and negative self-talk before the test.

Visualize.

Make a mental image of yourself taking the test. You know the answers and feel relaxed. Visualize doing well on the test and having no problems with the material. Visualizations can increase your confidence and decrease the anxiety you might otherwise feel before the test. Instead of thinking of this as a test, see it as an opportunity to demonstrate what you have learned!

Avoid negativity.

Worry is contagious and viral - once it gets started it builds on itself. Cut it off before it gets to be a problem. Even if you are relaxed and confident, being around anxious, worried classmates might cause you to start feeling anxious. Before the test, tune out the fears of classmates. Feeling anxious and worried before an exam is normal, and every student experiences those feelings at some point. But you cannot allow these feelings to interfere with your ability to perform well. Practicing mental preparation techniques and remembering that the test is not the only measure of your academic performance will ease your anxiety and ensure that you perform at your best.

How to Take a Test

EVERYONE KNOWS THAT TAKING AN EXAM IS STRESSFUL, BUT IT DOES NOT HAVE TO BE THAT BAD! There are a few simple things that you can do to increase your score on any type of test. Take a look at these tips and consider how you can incorporate them into your study time.

OK - so you are in the test room - Here is what to do!

Reading the Instructions

This is the most basic point, but one that, surprisingly, many students ignore and it costs big time! Since reading the instructions is one of the most common, and 100% preventable mistakes, we have a whole section just on reading instructions.

Pay close attention to the sample questions. Almost all standardized tests offer sample questions, paired with their correct solutions. Go through these to make sure that you understand what they mean and how they arrived at the correct answer. Do not be afraid to ask the test supervisor for help with a sample that confuses you, or instructions that you are unsure of.

Tips for Reading the Question

We could write pages and pages of tips just on reading the test questions. Here are a few that will help you the most.

- **Think first.** Before you look at the answer, read and think about the question. It is best to try to come up with the correct answer before you look at the options. This way, when the test-writer tries to trick you with a close answer, you will not fall for it.

- **Make it true or false.** If a question confuses you, then look at each answer option and think of it as a "true" "false" question. Select the one that seems most likely to be "true."

- **Mark the Question.** For some reason, a lot of test-takers are afraid to mark up their test booklet. Unless you are specifically told not to mark in the booklet, you should feel free to use it to your advantage.

- **Circle Key Words.** As you are reading the question, underline or circle key words. This helps you to focus on the most critical information needed to solve the problem. For example, if the question said, "Which of these is not a synonym for huge?" You might circle "not," "synonym" and "huge." That clears away the clutter and lets you focus on what is important.

- **Always underline these words:** all, none, always, never, most, best, true, false and except.

- **Eliminate.** Elimination is the best strategy for multiple choice answers *and* questions. If you are confused by lengthy questions, cross out anything that you think is irrelevant, obviously wrong, or information that you think is offered to distract you.

- **Do not try to read between the lines.** Usually, questions are written to be straightforward, with no deep, underlying meaning. Generally, the simple answer really is the correct answer. Do not over-analyze!

How to Take a Test - The Basics

Some sections of the test are designed to assess your ability to quickly grab the necessary information; this type of exam makes speed a priority. Others are more concerned with your depth of knowledge, and how accurate it is. When you start a new section of the test, look it over to determine whether the test is for speed or accuracy. If the test is for speed (a lot of questions and a short time), your strategy is clear; answer as many questions as quickly as possible.

The PAX does NOT penalize for wrong answers, so if all else fails, guess and make sure you answer every question.

Every little bit helps

The PAX does NOT allow personal calculators. You cannot bring any other materials into the test room. Scratch paper and a pencil are provided. Use them!

Make time your friend

Budget your time from the beginning until you are finished, and stick to it! The amount of time you are permitted for each portion of the test will almost certainly be included in the instructions.

Easy does it

One smart way to tackle a test is to locate the easy questions and answer those first. This is a time-tested strategy that never fails, because it saves you a lot of unnecessary anxiety. First, read the question and decide if you can answer it in less than a minute. If so, complete the question and go to the next one. If not, skip it for now and continue to the next question. By the time you have completed the first pass through this section of the exam, you will have answered a good number of questions. Not only does it boost your confidence, relieve anxiety and kick your memory up a notch, you will know exactly how many questions remain and can allot the rest of your time accordingly. Think of doing the easy questions first as a warm-up!

Do not watch your watch

At best, taking an important exam is an uncomfortable situation. If you are like most people, you might be tempted to subconsciously distract yourself from the task at hand. One of the most common ways to do so is by becoming obsessed with your watch or the wall clock. Do not watch your watch! Take it off and place it on the top corner of your desk, far enough away that you will not be tempted to look at it every two minutes. Better still, turn the watch face away from you. That way, every time you try to sneak a peek, you will be reminded to refocus your attention to the task at hand. Give yourself permission to check your watch or the wall clock after you complete each section.

Focus on answering the questions, not on how many minutes have elapsed since you last looked at it.

Divide and conquer

What should you do when you come across a question that is so complicated you may not even be certain what is being asked? As we have suggested, the first time through, skip the question. At some point, you will need to return to it and get it under control. The best way to handle questions that leave you feeling so anxious you can hardly think is by breaking them into manageable pieces. Solving smaller bits is always easier. For complicated questions, divide them into bite-sized pieces and solve these smaller sets separately. Once you understand what the reduced sections are really saying, it will be much easier to put them together and get a handle on the bigger question. This may not work with every question - see below for how to deal with questions you cannot break down.

Reason your way through the toughest questions

If you find that a question is so dense you can't figure out how to break it into smaller pieces, there are a few strategies that might help. First, read the question again and look for hints. Can you re-word the question in one or more different ways? This may give you clues. Look for words that can function as either verbs or nouns, and try to figure out what the questions is asking from the sentence structure. Remember that many nouns in English have several different meanings. While some of those meanings might be related, sometimes they are completely distinct. If reading the sentence one way does not make sense, consider a different definition or meaning for a key word.

The truth is, it is not always necessary to understand a question to arrive at a correct answer! The most successful strategy for multiple choice is Elimination. Frequently, at least one answer is clearly wrong and can be crossed off the list of possible correct answers. Next, look at the remaining answers and eliminate any that are only partially true. You may still have to flat-out guess from time to time, but using the process of elimination will help you make your way to the correct answer more often than not - even when you don't know what the question means!

Do not leave early

Use all the time allotted to you, even if you can't wait to get out of the testing room. Instead, once you have finished, spend the remaining time reviewing your answers. Go back to those questions that were most difficult for you and review your response. Another good way to use this time is to return to multiple-choice questions in which you filled in a bubble. Do a spot check, reviewing every fifth or sixth question to make sure your answer coincides with the bubble you filled in. This is a great way to catch yourself if you made a mistake, skipped a bubble and therefore put all your answers in the wrong bubbles!

Become a super sleuth and look for careless errors. Look for questions that have double negatives or other odd phrasing; they might be an attempt to throw you off. Careless errors on your part might be the result of skimming a question and missing a key word. Words such as "always," "never," "sometimes," "rarely" and the like can give a strong indication of the answer the question is really seeking. Don't throw away points by being careless!

Just as you budgeted time at the beginning of the test to allow for easy and more difficult questions, be sure to budget sufficient time to review your answers. On essay questions and math questions where you are required to show your work, check your writing to make sure it is legible.

Math questions can be especially tricky. The best way to double check math questions is by figuring the answer using a different method, if possible.

Here is another terrific tip. It is likely that no matter how hard you try, you will have a handful of questions you just are not sure of. Keep them in mind as you read through the rest of the test. If you can't answer a question, looking back over the test to find a different question that addresses the same topic might give you clues.

We know that taking the test has been stressful and you can hardly wait to escape. Just keep in mind that leaving before you double-check as much as possible can be a quick trip to disaster. Taking a few extra minutes can make the difference between getting a bad grade and a great one. Besides, there will be lots of time to relax and celebrate after the test is turned in.

In the Test Room – What you MUST do!

If you are like the rest of the world, there is almost nothing you would rather avoid than taking a test. Unfortunately, that is not an option if you want to pass. Rather than suffer, consider a few attitude adjustments that might turn the experience from a horrible one to…well, an interesting one! Take a look at these tips. Simply changing how you perceive the experience can change the experience itself.

You have to take the test - you can't change that. What you can change, and the only thing that you can change, is your attitude -so get a grip - you can do it!

Get in the mood

After weeks of studying, the big day has finally arrived. The worst thing you can do to yourself is arrive at the test site feeling frustrated, worried, and anxious. Keep a check on your emotional state. If your emotions are shaky before a test it can determine how well you do on the test. It is extremely important that you pump yourself up, believe in yourself, and use that confidence to get in the mood!

Don't fight reality

Students often resent tests, and with good reason. After all, many people do not test well, and they know the grade they end with does not accurately reflect their true knowledge. It is easy to feel resentful because tests classify students and create categories that just don't seem fair. Face it: Students who are great at rote memorization and not that good at actually analyzing material often score higher than those who might be more creative thinkers and balk at simply memorizing cold, hard facts. It may not be fair, but there it is anyway. Conformity is an asset on tests, and creativity is often a liability. There is no point in wasting time or energy being upset about this reality. Your first step is to accept the reality and get used to it. You will get higher marks when you realize tests do count and that you must give them your best effort. Think about your future and the career that is easier to achieve if you have consistently earned high grades. Avoid negative energy and focus on anything that lifts your enthusiasm and increases your motivation.

Get there early enough to relax

If you are wound up, tense, scared, anxious, or feeling rushed, it will cost you. Get to the exam room early and relax before you go in. This way, when the exam starts, you are comfortable and ready to apply yourself. Of course, you do not want to arrive so early that you are the only one there. That will not help you relax; it will only give you too much time to sit there, worry and get wound up all over again.

If you can, visit the room where you will be taking your exam a few days ahead of time. Having a visual image of the room can be surprisingly calming, because it takes away one of the big 'unknowns'. Not only that, but once you have visited, you know how to get there and will not be worried about getting lost. Furthermore, driving to the test site once lets you know how much time you need to allow for the trip. That means three potential stressors have been eliminated all at once.

Get it down on paper

One advantage of arriving early is that it allows you time to recreate notes. If you spend a lot of time worrying about whether you will be able to remember information like names, dates, places, and mathematical formulas, there is a solution for that. Unless the exam you are taking allows you to use your books and notes, (and very few do) you will have to rely on memory. Arriving early gives to time to tap into your memory and jot down key pieces of information you know that will be asked. Just make certain you are allowed to make notes once you are in the testing site; not all locations will permit it. Once you get your test, on a small piece of paper write down everything you are afraid you will forget. It will take a minute or two but by dumping your worries onto the page you have effectively eliminated a certain amount of anxiety and driven off the panic you feel.

Get comfortable in your chair

Here is a clever technique that releases physical stress and helps you get comfortable, even relaxed in your body. You will tense and hold each of your muscles for just a few seconds. The trick is, you must tense them hard for the technique to work. You might want to practice this technique a few times at home; you do not want an unfamiliar technique to add to your stress just before a test, after all! Once you are at the test site, this exercise can always be done in the rest room or another quiet location.

Start with the muscles in your face then work down your body. Tense, squeeze and hold the muscles for a moment or two. Notice the feel of every muscle as you go down your body. Scowl to tense your forehead, pull in your chin to tense your neck. Squeeze your shoulders down to tense your back. Pull in your stomach all the way back to your ribs, make your lower back tight then stretch your fingers. Tense your leg muscles and calves then stretch your feet and your toes. You should be as stiff as a board throughout your entire body.

Now relax your muscles in reverse starting with your toes. Notice how all the muscles feel as you relax them one by one. Once you have released a muscle or set of muscles, allow them to remain relaxed as you proceed up your body. Focus on how you are feeling as all the tension leaves. Start breathing deeply when you get to your chest muscles. By the time you have found your chair, you will be so relaxed it will feel like bliss!

Fight distraction

A lucky few are able to focus deeply when taking an important examination, but most people are easily distracted, probably because they would rather be any place else! There are a number of things you can do to protect yourself from distraction.

Stay away from windows.

If you select a seat near a window you may end gazing out at the landscape instead of paying attention to the work at hand. Furthermore, any sign of human activity, from a single individual walking by to a couple having an argument or exchanging a kiss will draw your attention away from your important work. What goes on outside should not be allowed to distract you.

Choose a seat away from the aisle so you do not become distracted by people who leave early. People who leave the exam room early are often the ones who fail. Do not compare your time to theirs.

Of course, you love your friends; that's why they are your friends! In the test room, however, they should become complete strangers inside your mind. Forget they are there. The first step is to physically distance yourself from friends or classmates. That way, you will not be tempted to glance at them to see how they are doing, and there will be no chance of eye contact that could either distract you or even lead to an accusation of cheating. Furthermore, if they are feeling stressed because they did not spend the focused time studying that you did, their anxiety is less likely to permeate your hard-earned calm.

Of course, you will want to choose a seat where there is sufficient light. Nothing is worse than trying to take an important examination under flickering lights or dim bulbs.

Ask the instructor or exam proctor to close the door if there is a lot of noise outside. If the instructor or proctor is unable to do so, block out the noise as best you can. Do not let anything disturb you.

The PAX does not allow any personal items in the exam room. Eat protein, complex carbohydrates and a little fat to keep you feeling full and to supercharge your energy.

Nothing is worse than a sudden drop in blood sugar during an exam.

Do not allow yourself to become distracted by being too cold or hot. Regardless of the weather outside, carry a sweater, scarf or jacket if the air conditioning at the test site is set too high, or the heat set too low. By the same token, dress in layers so that you are prepared for a range of temperatures.

Watch Caffeine

Drinking a gallon of coffee or gulping a few energy drinks might seem like a great idea, but it is, in fact, a very bad one. Caffeine, pep pills or other artificial sources of energy are more likely to leave you feeling rushed and ragged. Your brain might be clicking along, all right, but chances are good it is not clicking along on the right track! Furthermore, drinking lots of coffee or energy drinks will mean frequent trips to the rest room. This will cut into the time you should be spending answering questions and is a distraction in itself, since each time you need to leave the room you lose focus. Pep pills will only make it harder for you to think straight when solving complicated problems on the exam.

At the same time, if anxiety is your problem try to find ways around using tranquilizers during test-taking time. Even medically prescribed anti-anxiety medication can make you less alert and even decrease your motivation. Being motivated is what you need to get you through an exam. If your anxiety is so bad that it threatens to interfere with your ability to take an exam, speak to your doctor and ask for documentation. Many testing sites will allow non-distracting test rooms, extended testing time and other accommodations as long as a doctor's note that explains the situation is made available.

Keep Breathing

It might not make a lot of sense, but when people become anxious, tense, or scared, their breathing becomes shallow and, in some cases, they stop breathing all together! Pay attention to your emotions, and when you are feeling worried, focus on your breathing. Take a moment to remind yourself to breathe deeply and regularly. Drawing in steady, deep breaths energizes the body. When you continue to breathe deeply you will notice you exhale all the tension.

It is a smart idea to rehearse breathing at home. With continued practice of this relaxation technique, you will begin to know the muscles that tense up under pressure. Call these your "signal muscles." These are the ones that will speak to you first, begging you to relax. Take the time to listen to those muscles and do as they ask. With just a little breathing practice, you will get into the habit of checking yourself regularly and when you realize you are tense, relaxation will become second nature.

Avoid Anxiety Before a Test

Manage your time effectively

This is a key to your success! You need blocks of uninterrupted time to study all the pertinent material. Creating and maintaining a schedule will help keep you on track, and will remind family members and friends that you are not available. Under no circumstances should you change your blocks of study time to accommodate someone else, or cancel a study session to do something more fun. Do not interfere with your study time for any reason!

Relax

Use whatever works best for you to relieve stress. Some folks like a good, calming stretch with yoga, others find expressing themselves through journaling to be useful. Some hit the floor for a series of crunches or planks, and still others take a slow stroll around the garden. Integrate a little relaxation time into your schedule, and treat that time, too, as sacred.

Eat healthy

Instead of reaching for the chips and chocolate, fresh fruits and vegetables are not only yummy but offer nutritional benefits that help relieve stress. Some foods accelerate stress instead of reducing it and should be avoided. Foods that add to higher anxiety include artificial sweeteners, candy and other sugary foods, carbonated sodas, chips, chocolate, eggs, fried foods, junk foods, processed foods, red meat, and other foods containing preservatives or heavy spices. Instead, eat a bowl of berries and some yogurt!

Get plenty of ZZZZZZZs

Do not cram or try to do an all-nighter. If you created a study schedule at the beginning, and if you have stuck with that schedule, have confidence! Staying up too late trying to cram in last-minute bits of information is going to leave you exhausted the next day. Besides, whatever new information you cram in will only displace all the important ideas you've spent weeks learning. Remember: You need to be alert and fully functional the day of the exam

Have confidence in yourself!

Everyone experiences some anxiety when taking a test, but exhibiting a positive attitude banishes anxiety and fills you with the knowledge you really do know what you need to know. This is your opportunity to show how well prepared you are. Go for it!

Be sure to take everything you need

Depending on the exam, you may be allowed to have a pen or pencil, calculator, dictionary or scratch paper with you. Have these gathered together along with your entrance paperwork and identification so that you are sure you have everything that is needed.

Do not chitchat with friends

Let your friends know ahead of time that it is not anything personal, but you are going to ignore them in the test room! You need to find a seat away from doors and windows, one that has good lighting, and get comfortable. If other students are worried their anxiety could be detrimental to you; of course, you do not have to tell your friends that. If you are afraid they will be offended, tell them you are protecting them from your anxiety!

Common Test-Taking Mistakes

Taking a test is not much fun at best. When you take a test and make a stupid mistake that negatively affects your grade, it is natural to be very upset, especially when it is something that could have been easily avoided. So what are some of the common mistakes that are made on tests?

Do not fail to put your name on the test

How could you possibly forget to put your name on a test? You would be amazed at how often that happens. Very often, tests without names are thrown out immediately, resulting in a failing grade.

Marking the wrong multiple-choice answer

It is important to work at a steady pace, but that does not mean bolting through the questions. Be sure the answer you are marking is the one you mean to. If the bubble you need to fill in or the answer you need to circle is 'C', do not allow yourself to get distracted and select 'B' instead.

Answering a question twice

Some multiple-choice test questions have two very similar answers. If you are in too much of a hurry, you might select them both. Remember that only one answer is correct, so if you choose more than one, you have automatically failed that question.

Mishandling a difficult question

We recommend skipping difficult questions and returning to them later, but beware! First, be certain that you do return to the question. Circling the entire passage or placing a large question mark beside it will help you spot it when you are reviewing your test. Secondly, if you are not careful to skip the question, you can mess yourself up badly. Imagine that a question is too difficult and you decide to save it for later. You read the next question, which you know the answer, and you fill in that answer. You continue to the end of the test then return to the difficult question only to discover you didn't actually skip it! Instead, you inserted the answer to the following question in the spot reserved for the harder one, thus throwing off the remainder of your test!

Incorrectly Transferring an answer from scratch paper

This can happen easily if you are trying to hurry! Double check any answer you have figured out on scratch paper, and make sure what you have written on the test itself is an exact match!

Thinking too much

Oftentimes, your first thought is your best thought. If you worry yourself into insecurity, your self-doubts can trick you into choosing an incorrect answer when your first impulse was the right one!

Conclusion

CONGRATULATIONS! You have made it this far because you have applied yourself diligently to practicing for the exam and no doubt improved your potential score considerably! Passing your up-coming exam is a huge step in a journey that might be challenging at times but will be many times more rewarding and fulfilling. That is why being prepared is so important.

Good Luck!

Register for Free Updates and More Practice Test Questions

Register your purchase at

https://www.test-preparation.ca/register/ for fast and convenient access to updates, errata, free test tips and more practice test questions.

https://www.facebook.com/CompleteTestPreparation/

https://www.youtube.com/user/MrTestPreparation

Online Resources

How to Prepare for a Test - The Ultimate Guide

https://www.test-preparation.ca/prepare-test/

Learning Styles - The Complete Guide

https://www.test-preparation.ca/learning-style/

Test Anxiety Secrets!

https://www.test-preparation.ca/test-anxiety/

Time Management on a Test

https://www.test-preparation.ca/time-management/

Flash Cards - The Complete Guide

https://www.test-preparation.ca/flash-cards/

Test Preparation Video Series

https://www.test-preparation.ca/test-video/

How to Memorize - The Complete Guide

https://www.test-preparation.ca/memorize/

www.ingramcontent.com/pod-product-compliance
Lightning Source LLC
Chambersburg PA
CBHW070645160426
43194CB00009B/1581